THE (YOUNG)
MEN WE NEED

THE (YOUNG) MEN WE NEED

God's Purpose for Every Guy and How You Can Live It Out

BRANT HANSEN

BakerBooks

a division of Baker Publishing Group
Grand Rapids, Michigan

© 2024 by Brant Hansen

Published by Baker Books
a division of Baker Publishing Group
Grand Rapids, Michigan
BakerBooks.com

Some content in this book has been adapted from Brant Hansen, *The Men We Need: God's Purpose for the Manly Man, the Avid Indoorsman, or Any Man Willing to Show Up* (Grand Rapids: Baker Books, 2022).

Printed in the United States of America

Library of Congress Cataloging-in-Publication Data
Names: Hansen, Brant, 1969– author.
Title: The (young) men we need : God's purpose for every guy and how you can live it out / Brant Hansen.
Description: Grand Rapids, Michigan : Baker Books, a division of Baker Publishing Group, [2024] | Includes bibliographical references.
Identifiers: LCCN 2023029677 | ISBN 9781540903693 (paper) | ISBN 9781540903891 (casebound) | ISBN 9781493444113 (ebook)
Subjects: LCSH: Christian youth—Conduct of life. | Christian men. | Masculinity—Religious aspects—Christianity.
Classification: LCC BV4541.3 .H35 2024 | DDC 248.8/32—dc23/eng/20231004
LC record available at https://lccn.loc.gov/2023029677

The author is represented by the literary agency of The Gates Group.

To protect the privacy of those who have shared their stories with the author, some details and names have been changed.

Baker Publishing Group publications use paper produced from sustainable forestry practices and postconsumer waste whenever possible.

24 25 26 27 28 29 30   7 6 5 4 3 2 1

This book is dedicated to my stepdad, Carroll Smith.
Thank you for being the man I needed.

CONTENTS

Contents

Contents

Guys, we're waiting for you to do this, to BE this. We mean it. Make no mistake.

—Pretty Much Every Woman (paraphrase)

Here's a Very Important Introduction, So Hey, Don't Skip This

Thank you for reading this. Most people skip over introductions in these sorts of books. And by "most people," I mean me. But I need you to know a couple things from the outset.

First, I'm going to try to pack as much wisdom in this little book as possible. I don't want to waste your time.

Second, this book is split into two parts. The first part is to show you what "the young men we need" are like. The second part is about the six decisions you can make to become one of these men.

Ever since I wrote *The Men We Need*, I've been talking about it a lot. I've been speaking to big groups of people. Small groups too. And I've done a ton of interviews. A lot of the people in these groups, and a lot of the interviewees, have been women. When they hear the description of real masculinity that I'm going to spell out in this book, they have a very definite and emphatic reaction:

"YES! THAT'S IT! THAT'S WHO WE WANT MEN TO BE!"

It's *really* hard to get people to agree on something like this, or on anything, really. But I'm telling you—and you may not believe me, but it's true—that reaction has been unanimous so far. The message resonates with all ages, races, careers . . . and with women.

When people hear the description of real masculinity that I'm going to spell out in this book, they have a very definite and emphatic reaction: "YES! THAT'S IT! THAT'S WHO WE WANT MEN TO BE!"

That should tell us something.

Here's even better news: *This is something you can be.* It doesn't matter if you're a "manly man" or not. It doesn't matter how much you bench press or how awesome your facial hair is. You don't have to be jacked. You don't have to be a great hunter. You don't have to be great at starting a fire using only a rock or . . . whatever. You don't have to be rich or a mountain climber or a five-star football recruit.

All those things are great, but they're not at the core of what it *means* to be a man and what we're specifically designed to actually *do*. That's what this book is about.

There's something you need to know, and I need to get it out of the way early.

I play the accordion. I'm not good at grilling. I don't really enjoy camping. I was in Boy Scouts, but not successfully. I thought the other scouts would think I was "cool" if I brought my new flute to the campout. (Narrator: "But they did not think it was cool.")

That's right. I play the flute too. I wanted to play sports, but since I was always one of the smallest kids in the class, our town obsession—football—was a no-go. That is, until my senior year, when my mom finally agreed to let me play football after I had a growth spurt and shot up to my current five feet, ten inches.

Until I had to quit before the season started because (and I'm not making this up) *they couldn't find a helmet big enough for my head.*

I did use my oversized head successfully as captain of the Scholastic Bowl team, where I was all-conference. I was also the president— the *state* president—of the Illinois Student Librarians Association.

That's right. Let that soak in.

A little more about me. I'm pretty fit but not jacked. I have zero cool tattoos. I'm not against tats; it's just that I could never decide on one. I'm sure that if I did get one, it would be a *Lord of the Rings* character, but there are so many. I'd hate to go with Gandalf and then wish it was Gimli. I can't live with that kind of regret.

I respect hunters, but I don't hunt. I have a neurological condition called nystagmus that makes my eyes move back and forth rapidly, so in order to see, I have to move my head rapidly too. As you can imagine, rapid, involuntary head movement is not a plus for hunting with guns. It's not safe. Except for, you know, the animals. It's very safe for them.

I say all this because I want you to know this is not going to be one of those books that's all about how, if you want to be a *real* man, you've got to get out there and take down a moose using only judo moves or free-solo El Capitan. I can't do that stuff either.

I'm an avid indoorsman. I own puppets.

But you know what? As much as, say, climbing rocks is impressive and a fine sport, the world isn't truly desperate for more people who can climb rocks. Nothing against rock climbers; they're fantastic. It's also true that the world's deep longing isn't for more puppet-wielding accordion players. I've learned this repeatedly and emphatically.

If you do happen to be a jacked, tatted-up auto mechanic who spends his weekends hunting wild boar barehanded, I respect that. You're welcome here. This book is for you too.

But those things aren't at the heart of what people are yearning for from us. There's something much deeper and much better. That's what this book is about: the big vision for manhood.

The vision is this: *We men are at our best when we are functioning as protectors and defenders.* We are at our best when we champion the weak and vulnerable. We are at our best when we use whatever strength we have to safeguard the innocent. We are at our best when we do the job Adam was given: keeper of the garden.

You, and every other guy you know, can do this.

I should also let you know that this book is written by someone who believes in God. That, of course, is not an odd thing. What may be out of the ordinary is that God is not a side character in this play. He's the central one, influencing (I hope) every page. He knows us, what we're made for, and why we're here.

Our world is hurting. Here's hoping you become just the man we need.

THE KEEPER
OF THE GARDEN

The Poster

"What's the deal with the guy with the baby?"

I was asking this because a few of us were on a tour of a women's co-op house at the University of Illinois, where I was a student. And I kept seeing the same poster seemingly in everyone's room: a black-and-white photo of a guy in jeans with no shirt on, sitting and holding a baby. That's it.

Turns out that poster is one of the bestselling posters of all time, with more than five million sold.

But the guy doesn't seem *that* muscular or exceptional. You can't even see much of his face, really. He's a model, sure, but the world isn't short on models. So what's the deal? What made this poster so popular?

The student giving us the tour answered my question. "He's handsome, but it's not just the guy. It's the way the baby is looking at the guy."

Millions of women bought a poster because of the way a baby is looking at a guy? Yes, apparently.

"And the guy is cradling the baby's head. The baby is safe. We all want a guy like that."

Huh. As an eighteen-year-old guy who didn't have a girlfriend and had never had a girlfriend, I took note of this.

I mean, I knew I couldn't look like Poster Guy, but still.

For the record, this book isn't all about making yourself attractive to girls. It's about something much bigger, but it's worth noting how females often instinctually want to bring out the best in us.

There's a little experiment I've conducted several times while speaking to mixed groups of men and women or teenage girls and boys. I'll show photos from news stories of men helping people. Instead of a model, it's a soldier carrying an old woman out of a village, or two guys helping a family during a flood, or a guy pulling a baby out of an overturned car in a canal. Some of the men are overweight, some balding, some covered in filth. Nobody has ripped abs.

But it doesn't matter.

I'll ask a quick question of the women: "Do you find these men attractive?"

The response, without fail, is immediate: "YEEEEEEEESSSSS!!!"

I do this because I want the guys to feel the reaction and remember it like I remember Poster Guy. None of these guys look like what other guys would typically think women would freak out about, and yet, they freak out. Why?

Because these men are protectors. That's it.

Check out any survey of women being asked about the most attractive professions that men have. It's always the same: firefighters. Why? Because of pants with awesome reflectors?

No. It's not pants with reflectors. I've tried this.

It's because they rescue people. They take responsibility for the vulnerable.

Now, you can use this information to decide, "Hey, I'm going to be a firefighter so women will like me." But the bigger and better takeaway is this: *Women sense who we are supposed to be.* And yes, they are attracted to us when they see us living that out. They're looking for men who make them feel secure. This is why women often consider confidence, a fit body, wealth, or a deep voice "sexy." Wise women, of course, know these are mere surface indicators and can be misleading to the extreme . . . but they're certainly hoping.

Please know this: A man who is a confident provider and protector can be less than wealthy. He can have a high-pitched voice. He can be less than fit . . . and still be very attractive to women.

Fun fact: Apparently, sometimes you don't even have to do anything to be admired for being an attractive man of action. A few nights ago, a group of loud teenage guys was in the street in front of our house after 11:00. They didn't bother me, so I sprang into inaction and stayed in bed.

But my wife, Carolyn, was very unsettled. She couldn't sleep and watched them through the window. She went downstairs. I didn't understand what the big deal was. But I finally got out of bed.

I got dressed, went downstairs, and headed out the door to confront the guys. But as I walked out the door, they all left. I didn't even do anything. And Carolyn's reaction?

I'm super hot. That's what. I did nothing, and suddenly my attractiveness made a quantum jump.

Wait, I *did* do something. I showed a willingness to act. A *willingness* to intervene on my wife's behalf. My wife is not a fearful person, and she didn't marry me for my awesome nunchuck skills. But women love it when we prove we're *willing* to do what needs to be done. It turns out it's not about muscle at all but about character.

> **Women love it when we prove we're *willing* to do what needs to be done. It turns out it's not about muscle at all but about character.**

In fact, if you prove to be a man who is passive or weak in character, a woman who was once attracted to your ripped muscles will ultimately begin to resent those same ripped muscles. You will simply lose her respect, no matter how much you work out.

Women sense when we are fulfilling our purpose and when we're not. Not only do they lack respect for passive men, but they resent them. They know men are made for something more, and that "more" is a signpost, I believe, pointing us to something: our purpose. What women want from us looks exactly like what God created Adam to do in the Bible's account of the garden of Eden.

I'm hoping that by the time you've finished this book, you have a deep sense of that purpose. If you do, the vulnerable people around you—and maybe those far away—will flourish because of it.

Adam left his post, and the world has been suffering ever since. The world is yearning for men who show up. All kinds of men, in all walks of life, who know who they are and why they are here . . . and don't leave.

The world needs us to show up. You ready for this?

Masculinity Is about Taking Responsibility

"Is this the best a man can get? Is it?"

That's a voiceover in an ad Gillette debuted in 2019. The ad showed men behaving badly, preying on women, and acting as bullies.

But then the ad pivots:

> But something finally changed. Because . . . we believe in the best in men. To say the right thing. To act the right way. Some already are. . . . But some is not enough. Because the boys watching today will be the men of tomorrow.[1]

The images illustrating the "act the right way" theme are of men intervening to break up fights or stopping other men from making women feel threatened. There is also a great image of a dad holding his little daughter in front of a mirror, telling her that she's strong.

The ad was a hit. And while our culture is extremely confused about masculinity, I'm convinced that, deep down, almost everyone gets it. They know that the purpose of masculine strength is to protect, and when we fulfill our role, we're truly at our best.

This expectation goes back in history quite a few years. Like . . . all the way to Adam: "Then the LORD God took the man and put him in the garden of Eden to tend and keep it" (Gen. 2:15 NKJV).

The Hebrew word translated "keep" here is *shamar*. It means "to guard," "to protect," and "to watch over."[2]

Guard. Protect. Watch over. (Of course, Adam totally blew it, but we'll get to that soon enough.)

Think about what the garden of Eden was: a place that God and humans would inhabit together. A place at peace. A place that was wildly beautiful and where things were made to thrive and to grow.

But it wasn't finished. It wasn't a dollhouse or a retirement village. There was work to do. It needed guarding and cultivating and ordering. God created man and woman in his image, and that means they were made to be creative and actually *do* things that matter.

So God gave Adam the job of looking after this place and the things within it. He was to guard it, tend it, and help it flourish. He was responsible for it.

Masculinity is about taking responsibility. We respect men who take responsibility for themselves. We have even more respect for those who go beyond themselves to their families. And we have immense respect for men who take responsibility for those well outside their own homes.

> We are "masculine" not to the extent that we body-build or achieve sexual conquests or fix stuff, but to the extent that we are faithful to the job of being humble keepers of the garden.

We are "masculine" not to the extent that we body-build or achieve sexual conquests or fix stuff, but to the extent that we are faithful to the job of being humble keepers of the garden. Just as Adam's failure was devastating, the continued failure of men to fill this role has been devastating for our entire world.

When we do fulfill our purpose, we become a source of life for those around us. The vulnerable will be allowed to grow and bloom. People will sense that they're safe around us. Our schools, neighborhoods, workplaces, and homes will be safer simply because we're there. (Of course, not *everyone* will feel so safe. If we are who we are made to be, those who want to attack the garden or who would threaten those within will not feel secure at all. Our mere presence will bother them.)

Keepers of the garden don't need to be physical brutes. What we do need is the willingness to bring whatever resources we have to fill this role wherever we are.

We need to remind ourselves why we're here and who we need to be. Then we need to live it out.

━━ ━━ ━━ ━━

Please understand this: The original garden was a place where God was fully in charge. He was King, and his justice and peace were present, to everyone's benefit. We were supposed to rule with him and to expand his rule, but we misused our freedom.

We get to be part of expanding that kingdom here and now in the places we find ourselves. Not as a power move—quite the opposite! We do it through humility.

You were made to do this, whether you're a top student, musician, motorcycle mechanic, or a drive-through worker at Burger King. Maybe you're a fellow nerd like me, or maybe you can squat six hundred pounds. Doesn't matter.

Maybe you're outwardly healthy; maybe you're battling an obvious disability. Doesn't matter.

Wealthy or poor? Makes no difference.

We're all called to be keepers and protectors in our spheres of influence, whatever and wherever those spheres are.

The way Jesus explains the kingdom of God (and he talks about it more than anything else in the Gospels), it works very differently from how we understand the world. The weak are made strong. The last are first. The humble are exalted. The proud are brought low. The widow and the orphan are valued highly. The unfairly treated are defended. Things are set right. The seemingly insignificant go to the head of the class. The lost are found. And the broken are healed.

Imagine men like you and me taking whatever strength or talent we are given to defend and expand that kingdom, rather than being sidetracked with our own little throwaway ones that will never last.

Imagine if we approached life like this: "Adam didn't take responsibility as a protector. But with whatever I have, I'm going to do it. I have a mission, and I accept it."

Jesus told us to seek God's kingdom first. When we do, it's not just good news for us. It's good news for everyone around us.

We Need You Out Here, Man

This brings us to the "Jake question." It's a fun one to bat around with people.

Let's say "Jake" is a relatively physically healthy twenty-year-old. He lives with his parents and stays inside almost all day, every day. He spends his time playing video games and watching porn while his parents provide meals and snacks.

He's content. He'd say he's happy with his life.

Is this okay? I mean, is there anything really "wrong" with this? He's happy. He's not bothering or harming anyone else.

Is there actually a problem?

For some, the answer will be obvious: no. There really isn't a problem at all because if he's not hurting anyone else and he's happy, what does it matter?

But that reasoning doesn't quite work because it ignores this fact: Jake *is* actually harming someone. He's harming himself and others by not being who he was created to be.

The world needs Jake. There are real humans outside Jake's window who will suffer because he isn't who we need him to be. There are perhaps dozens of people, maybe thousands, whose lives will be worse because Jake is a no-show.

Also, he may currently be "happy," but who says that mere happiness is the end goal? After all, it can and will be fleeting.

Maybe we should pursue something bigger and richer and longer lasting than that.

Now, Jake may not look like a typical hero, but he could decide to be one. Like all of us, he has been given a measure of strength and intelligence and creativity. God has given him what he needs to do the things that need to be done in this world. We'll talk more about those things, but these are worth thinking about now:

While Jake accomplishes tasks in fake worlds, there are things that need to be done in the real world.

While he entertains himself with images of women, there are real women yearning for actual grown-up men.

While his games and entertainment may center on fake storylines of fighting injustice, there are real people who need protection.

Everything Jake has is given to him for a reason, including his freedom. It really is up to him whether he chooses life through the real or death through the fake.

He's like all of us. This is where we are right now. This Jake, like the original Adam, was created to be a keeper of the garden, a protector and defender. He was created to bring order from chaos. He was created to make the things and people around him thrive and grow in beauty and strength.

But he's AWOL.

It's simply not enough to say about your life, "I didn't bother anybody." You were created to take responsibility. You will thrive if you grow into that purpose.

In fact, I'd argue this: If a grown-up male's life is all about, say, entertainment options, using women for sexual pleasure, smoking weed, and modifying his car, he's not a man. He's stuck in boy-dom. God loves him dearly, yes, and there are people rooting for him, sure. But he's not the man the world needs him to be.

Not yet. Wow, do we need him to grow up.

Some boys start becoming men early. Some are told when they're little that they have a role. I remember when my son was picking on his little sister. Justice was nine, and Julia was six. I told him, "Justice, you are supposed to be her protector. Instead, you're being a threat. You are betraying your job!"

Even at that age he understood this very clearly, and he took it to heart. Honestly, I don't remember him ever picking on his sister again!

Young kids can understand this role. It's sad that they, and even adult men, don't often hear it. We all very much want mission and purpose, whether we realize it or not. We become distorted without them. We get caught up more easily in the things that make us shrink and wither.

The great thing is that God will use any of us who are willing to show up.

Jake, we need you out here.

Toxic Passivity and
the Original Guy

The term "toxic masculinity" is used a lot, and it's understandable why. There are too many guys who try to dominate the vulnerable, using power or even violence to try to control people. Hopefully, you'll see in this book why that's a betrayal of what real masculinity is.

But there's another kind of "toxic" when it comes to us guys: toxic passivity. It may not seem like it, but toxic passivity is as threatening as its counterpart.

For example, you may have observed this in married couples: a husband can make his wife feel less secure if she suspects he won't defend her, their relationship, or their home. Maybe he's mentally or emotionally checked out and doesn't seem to care. Maybe he just stays quiet and passively accepts whatever happens around him. She may feel like she's somewhat on her own, even though they're married. She may have to use enormous energy to cover all of life's bases because he may not do it.

It's very unsettling, and you know what? It's everywhere.

My friends Paul and Virginia Friesen are PhDs and family counselors. They say passive men are a far more common problem in their practice than men who are overbearing, physically intimidating, or the other traits we assign to toxic masculinity.

We know we don't want to be like this. Nobody admires a passive man. People don't buy movie tickets to watch men without a mission. There is no Whatever Man hero in the Marvel Universe.

Passive Man is a disappointment at best and a threat at worst. Don't be him or his underperforming fellow superhero, Blaming Guy. No one respects him either.

In the Bible, Adam managed to be both. God told him to tend and keep the garden. It was one of the very first things he'd ever told a man to do.

We've talked about what "keep" means. And the Hebrew word *abad* that's translated "tend" also carries deep meaning. It's a verb that means to do work as a servant, even a worshiper.

So God gives Adam his assignment: protect and cultivate and watch over. Do it as a worshiper, someone who partners with God in his life's work. Then he tells Adam not to eat from the tree of the knowledge of good and evil.

Later, God creates Eve, a "suitable helper" for Adam. Some men read that and think, *See? Women are our underlings.* But that doesn't accurately capture what it means at all.

The word for "helper" is *ezer*. God himself is described as *ezer* in Psalms. He's our helper because he has the ability to help us in our need. He rescues us because we need rescuing. He is not our inferior. But you knew that.

Women were to be corulers with men from the very start. In Genesis 1, God creates mankind in his own image, "male and female" (v. 27), and then he blesses them and tells them to be fruitful, increase in number, and rule over the earth. Again, that's not just for the man. We are distinctly different, yes, but male and female are made to rule together.

Then Eve has a conversation in the garden with an enemy of God. The enemy claims she's missing out on some greater power and knowledge by obeying the command God gave to Adam.

She fears she's missing out and falls for the lie. She eats the forbidden fruit. And all the while, Adam does something remarkable: *absolutely nothing.*

When I heard this story as a kid, I always pictured Adam far away, doing some hard work elsewhere in the garden while Eve was dealing with the snaky enemy. But notice where Adam actually is:

> When the woman saw that the fruit of the tree was good for food and pleasing to the eye, and also desirable for gaining wisdom, she took some and ate it. She also gave some to her husband, *who was with her,* and he ate it. Then the eyes of both of them were opened, and they realized they were naked; so they sewed fig leaves together and made coverings for themselves. (Gen. 3:6–7, italics mine)

It sounds like he's right there with her! Adam lets Eve talk with an enemy of God, and he does nothing to protect her or the garden.

Adam is so passive he doesn't even grab any fruit for himself. Eve passes it to him. Maybe he's lying down?

Whatever he's doing, it's a betrayal of who he is supposed to be. He's supposed to guard the garden, but he just stands there—or maybe sits or lies there—while the world takes a blow we still haven't recovered from.

Then this happens:

> The man and his wife heard the sound of the LORD God as he was walking in the garden in the cool of the day, and they hid from the LORD God among the trees of the garden. But the LORD God called to the man, "Where are you?"
>
> He answered, "I heard you in the garden, and I was afraid because I was naked; so I hid." (vv. 8–10)

So the woman eats the fruit first and receives all the blame for this for thousands of years. But God never calls *her* out by name. No. He wants to know where Adam is.

Just to review a bit:

When the garden was faced with a threat, Adam did nothing.

When Eve was under spiritual attack, Adam did nothing.

When Eve offered him fruit, Adam took the path of least resistance.

When God came into the garden to speak to him, Adam hid.

At no point in this story is Adam doing his job. He is passive.

He was not created to be passive. Humans were not created to evade responsibility, hide from God, or make up excuses and deflect blame.

Where are you, Adam?

Now, to be sure, Adam and Eve are both in trouble. The fact that God comes looking for Adam doesn't mean he's more significant than Eve. But God's question is, "Where's the keeper of the garden? Where's the one I made to take responsibility?"

As I look around at how few guys are truly showing up, it may be that he's still asking.

The Ancient Art of
Blaming Other People

Back to Genesis. When Adam fails to do his job, he deals with it like most of us tend to deal with things: He finds somebody else to blame.

Since there's only one other person around, I guess the choice is easy. It's *that woman*.

The LORD God called to the man, "Where are you?"

He answered, "I heard you in the garden, and I was afraid because I was naked; so I hid."

And he said, "Who told you that you were naked? Have you eaten from the tree that I commanded you not to eat from?"

The man said, "*The woman you put here with me*—she gave me some fruit from the tree, and I ate it." (Gen. 3:9–12, italics mine)

Let's think about this. Here's what we know:

Genesis was written thousands of years ago.

It tells the story of the first man.

The first time the first man does something wrong, he blames someone else.

Sounds . . . believable. This is how humans roll.

What Adam does is especially jarring when we remember his very first reaction to woman: He totally falls for her. He even gets poetic about her. His first words—the first words of the first man in the Bible!—are like a love song about the wonder of this magnificent creature, this "woman"!

And then his next words? Blaming that magnificent creature. Adam pivots from describing her this way:

> This is now bone of my bones
>   and flesh of my flesh;
> she shall be called "woman,"
>   for she was taken out of man. (Gen. 2:23)

To blaming her this way:

The woman you put here with me. (Gen. 3:12)

That's quite a transition. "Oh, the rapture! She is my flesh! We are one! United forever and ev— Wait, what? THAT WOMAN DID IT."

Notice that the first man pulls off an impressive Double Blame Move. He's also blaming God for putting "the woman" there in the first place.

As I've said, the guys we need are those who take responsibility. What we don't need is yet more excuse making, but we do it all the time, in ways both subtle and obvious.

Allow me an obvious example, in the form of a provocative question for people who are Jesus followers:

Q: A very attractive woman wears a dress that is revealing. A man nearby decides to fantasize about having sex with her. Who's at fault for his decision?

(A) She is.

(B) He is.

(C) Mostly him, but she's culpable too because she shouldn't be wearing stuff like that.

(D) Neither, because there's nothing wrong with the man's fantasy, and Jesus never really emphasized this sort of thing or talked about it. We should focus on real issues.

I will give you the correct answer.

It's B. He's at fault. Completely.

A, C, and D are all excuses.

D is especially dangerous because it uses a false claim—that Jesus didn't talk about lust or regard it as a "real issue"—to provide an excuse. He certainly did talk about lust, and the entire Bible is full of both warnings about it and examples of the devastating effects of it.

A and C are wrong because the woman is not at fault. It's not even 90/10. She's not at fault at all.

"But," you might say, "she shouldn't dress that way."

"But," I would respond, "that wasn't the question, was it?" The question was about who is ultimately responsible for the *man's* behavior, and the answer is . . . the *man.*

You and I are 100 percent responsible for whether we decide to fantasize about someone. That's our call. Please know, I'm not saying noticing that a woman is extremely attractive is lust. Noticing is not an act of will. But engaging our imagination is. We can look away, and we can move our minds to other distractions, if we so choose.

This is on us. Is it difficult, if you're in a habit of getting a sexual "buzz" from looking at women? Yes, it is. But it's not at all impossible. Again, we're not talking about merely noticing or even appreciating a woman's attractiveness. We're talking about our decisions from there.

Don't do the Double Blame Move. Don't do the "It's that woman" thing. Own it.

None of this is a guilt trip. It's actually good news. We're not helpless victims in life, at the mercy of whoever walks by or whatever's on the next billboard. We don't *have* to lust. We *can* take our thoughts captive. It's true.

Again, I'm just using this as an example. There are so many ways we try to shift blame to someone else. But if we're not blame shifters, we'll be refreshing to people. Taking responsibility is such a rare but impactful thing.

You have the responsibility of guarding your heart. *You* have the say in whether you will allow God to shape who you are becoming. No one else will do this for you.

You have the responsibility of guarding your heart. You have the say in whether you will allow God to shape who you are becoming. No one else will do this for you.

And this is great news. It means that if you intend to be the man God created you to be and the man we need you to be, you can do so. That goal is not out of reach. It's not up to others.

I love this quote from habit expert James Clear:

> A profitable business is never a choice, it is a series of choices.
> A fit body is never a choice, it is a series of choices.
> A strong relationship is never a choice, it is a series of choices.[1]

You make choices. They matter. They are yours. Yes, some of your choices will be selfish, immature, and foolish. But own them. Learn and grow from them.

Continue to bring your attention back to God (we'll talk about this later), and watch how he changes you over time to become the sort of person who more naturally chooses the right things, the wise things. Those are the things that give life to you and everyone else in your garden.

A Tale of Two Men . . .
and Every Woman

There's a video you really need to look up on YouTube.[1] Rarely do we get such a vision of two possible futures so beautifully and starkly laid out before us.

There are two men in the video, which was taken with someone's phone on a street in France.

> Guy #1: An immigrant from Mali. We can't see his face. What we can see is him boldly scaling a building. Why is he scaling a building? He sees a child dangling from a high balcony. He attacks the problem. He uses every bit of his strength and endurance to successfully rescue the little four-year-old boy.
>
> Guy #2: The four-year-old's dad. Oh, wait. He's not in the video. He's nowhere to be seen. Why is he nowhere to be seen while his child's life hangs in the balance? He wasn't paying attention. He was playing Pokémon.

Remember this and take it to heart: Every woman in the world admires Guy #1. Every woman thinks that what he just did is very, very attractive.

But what does he look like? We can't tell. Doesn't matter.

What kind of car does he drive? Again, doesn't matter.

How ripped are his abs? No one cares. He's attractive because of what he's doing.

Also remember this: Every woman in the world thinks Guy #2 is a loser who needs to grow up.

Maybe he's handsome and drives a Maserati. Doesn't matter. Why?

Because every woman loves a man who takes responsibility. Guy #2 doesn't take responsibility. He is Passive Man.

Guy #1 takes responsibility not only for himself but for someone he doesn't even know. Again, taking responsibility is the very essence of masculinity.

In Jesus, of course, we get a brilliant example of masculinity in so many ways. (We'll talk later about Jesus' master class on how to treat women.) He is described as the second Adam, the one we need who takes responsibility for the world. He's the absolute opposite of passive.

> **Taking responsibility is the very essence of masculinity.**

Let's recap:

Every woman admires a man who does things in real life.

She is not impressed by a man who rescues an entire virtual division in *Call of Duty*.

She is very impressed by a man who is willing to risk his own life for the right cause.

Every woman loves a man who rises above the crowd of do-nothings. Guy #1 does this literally, of course. But think about it. He wasn't the only one who saw that kid dangling. He was just the only one who said, "I'm fixing this."

"But Brant," you say. "These are really big blanket statements. 'Every woman . . .'? Really? You can't say that!"

"But this is my book, and I totally can," I reply. "Yes, there is probably one woman who hates men who rescue children, and yes, she will leave a bitter review of this awesome book on Amazon, but I'm saying it anyway."

And here's another big blanket statement that's worth remembering the rest of your life: *A man whose primary "heroism" is virtual is not the best version of the man he could have been.*

You can be Guy #1 or Guy #2.

No one can make that decision for you.

It's your call.

Don't Be Afraid of Commitments—Be Afraid of *Not* Making Commitments

We love keeping our options open. We live in the time of options. Most humans haven't lived like this, but for us, it's hard to imagine living any other way.

But the truth is our neighbors and communities need men who *don't* keep their options open. They need men who commit. That means making choices that cut off other options.

How do we do that in a world filled with so many options? We can't be restricted to just the option of, say, having potato chips. We need choices! We need them in big bags, in small bags, and stacked in cylinders.

And we won't be stuck with just one kind of cylinder chip either. Pringles alone gives us the options of BBQ, Cheddar Cheese, Cheddar & Sour Cream, French Onion Dip, Honey Mustard, and Jalapeño. There is also Loaded Baked Potato, Memphis BBQ (not to be confused with non-Memphis BBQ), Pizza, Salt & Vinegar, Ranch, Sour Cream & Onion, Nacho Cheese, and Southwestern Ranch.

And if we feel limited by this selection, we can opt for Fiery Sweet BBQ (also not from Memphis), Screamin' Dill Pickle, and

Tangy Buffalo Wing. There are the lightly salted, reduced fat, and fat-free options as well. Plus Cheeseburger flavor. And Chili Con Queso. The list goes on and on. In fact, there are thirty-four different kinds of Pringles. I counted them.

The point is, we are used to being consumers, constantly evaluating our ever-expanding options and looking for upgrades. It's a way of life. But always keeping our options open is a disastrous way to live when it comes to the things that matter.

It's good to decide. Of course, "decide" is a very final word, and a lot of us try to avoid decision making. To decide literally means "to cut off" and comes from the same root word as "incisors" and "scissors."

Commitment means closing certain doors in order to choose and step through a better one. It means embracing our limits, acknowledging that we can't be everywhere, do everything, or be with everybody at once.

If we don't make decisions, if we don't embrace our limits, we will achieve nothing. It's that simple.

Want to be a world-class neurosurgeon? You probably won't be simultaneously on the PGA Tour.

Want to have deep, everyday relationships with your neighbors in Portland? You won't be able to live in Oslo.

Want to be an epic father who's remembered fondly for generations for his impact on his friends and family? You won't be able to travel fifty weeks a year for your job.

Want to be a great husband? You'll have to choose not to flirt with other women.

That's how it works. Anything truly poetic we experience in life will be the result of embracing limits. Remaining a free agent forever might seem sexy, but it's a surefire ticket to loneliness. There are things you are free to experience only if you fully commit and cut off other options.

I've been married thirty-plus years. If I had kept my options open, I would not know what it's like to have a woman know me this well and still love me. I only get to experience the freedom of this kind of love because I didn't opt for other things or people.

If I'd kept all my options open in life, I would not know what it's like to walk my daughter down the aisle. But now I do.

If I'd kept all my options open in life, I would not know what it's like to pin a military officer's insignia on my son. I've gotten to live alongside this man every single step of the way, from crying infant to combat medal recipient.

Remaining a free agent forever might seem sexy, but it's a surefire ticket to loneliness. There are things you are free to experience only if you fully commit and cut off other options.

Our daughter and her husband are now parents. Being a new grandpa is fantastic. I see that baby girl nearly every day, and I love it. If I'd kept all my options open in life, I'd have missed out on that too.

I admit I really didn't know what I was doing when I got married. I'm not sure anyone does. It's too profound to fully take in. I didn't know how it would turn out. I didn't know how I'd be pushed to change and grow. I didn't know all the costs and benefits.

But I did know this: I was choosing this woman and cutting off all other options. So much of the beauty in my life has flowed from that decision.

We love staying open and available to a better option that might present itself. It's human. (Adam and Eve fell for this kind of thinking.) But that's not how real freedom is found. We find more freedom when we bind ourselves to the *right* things—to life-giving things and things that *last*.

I'm not saying you have to get married to experience the fulfillment that comes with commitment. But it's not good for a man to be alone, and relationships are built on commitment.

I suppose I'll always struggle with regrets about this or that dumb thing I've done. But I promise you that when I'm on my deathbed, I won't look back and think, *You know, I should've kept all my options open.*

No, I'll remember the look in my daughter's eyes and how pretty she was on a spring day as I walked with her in the dappled sunshine. And when I was asked the question, "Who gives this woman to be wed?" I got the chance to say, "Her mother and I do." Because I made a decision, and I never looked back.

THE SIX DECISIONS THAT WILL SET YOU APART

Now that we've talked about what it means to be a keeper of the garden, we're going to talk about how to do it.

These six decisions will be critical in determining the direction of your life. And not just your life, as it turns out. If you choose to live this way, you won't just stand out. You'll be a source of life for everyone around you.

FORSAKE THE FAKE
AND
RELISH THE REAL

The Big Swindle

Ever get ripped off?

This is going to sound especially dumb—I'm being vulnerable here—but we got ripped off during the COVID-19 quarantine. Everybody was hogging all the toilet paper around town, so we outflanked them (seriously apologizing for that pun, but I'm leaving it here, so am I *really* sorry?) and ordered some on Amazon—twelve rolls for forty bucks.

When they arrived, there were twelve rolls, all right: twelve remarkably tiny rolls, rolls for elves. All twelve rolls could fit in a shoebox. I laughed, until I realized, "Okay, but seriously. We still need some toilet paper."

Yes, I fell for the ol' Tiny Toilet Paper Swindle, which brings to mind an important Chinese book, *The Book of Swindles*. I'm not really an expert on this book (I just found out about it while googling ten minutes ago), but it's about twenty-four different kinds of swindles, and it was written in the 1600s.

Reviewers say it's quite relevant for today. This is because, while technology has developed over the centuries, humans haven't changed that much. We're always falling for things. We're convinced we're getting one thing and wind up with another.

Adam and Eve come back to mind. They got swindled. And then there's this from about 2,700 years ago:

Food gained by fraud tastes sweet,
  but one ends up with a mouth full of gravel. (Prov. 20:17)

There are two reasons this proverb is beautiful. First, because you absolutely need to name your next hip-hop/acoustic neo-punk band "Mouth of Gravel." But you already knew this.

And second, it's just so true.

Fraudulent gains taste sweet—at first. Then there's a dark turn, and we're left with bitterness and pain. That's how sin works. Always promising, initially exciting, this rush of freedom . . . and then the punch in the gut.

Of course, when Adam and Eve got swindled, they were promised something, and it seemed to them like a better plan than what God was offering. So they went for it. The fruit tasted very sweet at first, but . . . not for long.

Think about how we commonly destroy our lives based on some version of this swindle. Few people have this plan: "I'm going to get addicted to this [substance or activity], and I'm going to destroy my life and family with it."

No, it always starts with excitement, with a burst of what feels like something life-giving, and then . . . you know, mouth full of gravel.

And you're by yourself.

The enemy—a swindler from the beginning—has a plan: Isolate us. He won't advertise it that way. Isolation never seems to be the goal, but it's always the end result.

And then there's Jesus, who "is before all things, and in him all things hold together," Paul writes in Colossians 1:17. God's plan is for things to come together, under his authority. Real life leads us toward each other, not away.

━━ ━━ ━━ ━━

Yuri Tolochko is a bodybuilder who looks like an action hero. He's massively muscular with a full, manly beard. He also "married" a sex doll. Apparently, there are conflicts in his relationship

with the lifeless toy, like when he "forbade her from Instagram."
He said, "Maybe I'm being too selfish. But that's the beauty of
Margo, that I can do this to her and she won't mind."[1]

Exactly. This "woman" isn't a woman, and he is not the man
we need him to be.

At the time of this writing, the sale of sex dolls and robots
is booming. *Forbes* magazine reported a spike of 51 percent in
just one two-month period in 2020. "We have lots of products in
stock but we can't work fast enough to keep up with demand,"
one company founder said.[2]

One robot-selling company says the driver behind the sales isn't
just sexual pleasure. It's *connection*. "We have combined the best
features of the female mind and body. . . . This means not only can
you enjoy their sexuality, but you can also connect with her on a
human intimate level. She will emanate comfort and safety from
her warm body allowing the intimacy to grow over time." Your
robot will tell you the weather, ask about your day, and help you
"have the mental stimulation you have always craved."[3]

Looks real. Acts real, even empathetic. Makes you feel like
you have an "intimate" relationship that the manufacturers know
you're really yearning for. Provides you with a dopamine hit.

And after it's over, after you've tricked your own brain and
body parts, it's just you and yourself and some plastic. That's it.

Just you. Again. By yourself.

It's a con job designed to destroy you. This fake has the veneer
of womanhood, of companionship, but can't call you out to take
responsibility. The fake never calls you out to be the man we need
you to be.

"The best features of the female mind . . ." That's another lie
within the lie. A real woman's mind adds to us, challenges us, com-
plements us, confounds us, confronts us, and makes us grow up.

Funny how handing ourselves over to our own desires always
ultimately leaves us in the same place. God created us for relationship, but we get swindled into isolation.

This is how sin operates. It's sly. It's a replacement. It substitutes a good thing for something ultimately hollow. It promises life but delivers a death blow.

Our sin isn't sin because it's on a random list of activities that God just doesn't happen to like. Sin is sin because it destroys us.

Pornography and sex with plastic are the obvious examples of taking something great, something beautifully life-giving and relational, and then, abraca-presto—turning it into soul-killing loneliness.

Remember this: Our sin isn't sin because it's on a random list of activities that God just doesn't happen to like. Sin is sin because it destroys us. God is on our side. He doesn't want anything to stop us from being who we're supposed to be.

Let's Talk about
"Supernormal" Traps

Honestly, I feel sorry for us. It's not supposed to be this difficult.

I think you and I are up against circumstances the likes of which men of previous generations haven't faced. For centuries, there's been wisdom literature (like Proverbs 5) warning men against destroying their lives by giving in to disordered sexual desire. But there has never before been a time when we can so easily get drawn into something as dangerous as "supernormal stimulation." And it's worth talking about because it can destroy everything in your life.

Some famous research on this topic was conducted by Nikolaas Tinbergen, who should be saluted for being (1) a Nobel Prize winner and (2) the person with seriously the most Dutch-sounding name of all time. He sounds like a guy who, every Christmas, climbs down your windmill to give you ice skates.

Anyway, he wanted to find out if birds would prefer to sit on fake eggs if the eggs had more defined markings, had more color, or were bigger. And they did! The exaggerated eggs were hard to resist.[1]

Tinbergen also wanted to find out if a particular territorial fish—the male stickleback—would more aggressively attack a rival fish if the rival's underside was redder than usual. He made some fake wooden stickleback fish and painted their undersides an exaggerated bright red. The real fish attacked in a frenzy. The redder the fish, the more aggressive the reaction.

Then Tinbergen wondered about sexual attraction in butterflies. He constructed a fake female butterfly out of cardboard. The model was rudimentary and unrealistic, but he gave it the exaggerated markings of female butterflies, using more vivid colors. Would the males be more attracted to the fake, exaggerated female?

You bet they were! They tried to mate with the fake butterfly. They were entranced. Beautiful, real females waited nearby . . . but they couldn't compete. They had no chance. They were now ignored.

When it came to stimulation, the real simply couldn't compete with the exaggerated fake.

Sound familiar?

We humans have the same problem. We'll go for the exaggerated fake, and we lose our appetite for the real. This desire is distorted, of course, but it's not the deepest tragedy here.

The deepest tragedy is that giving in to our desire for the fake distorts *us*. Psychologically. Sexually. Even physically.

We become less real, less human.

"Supernormal stimuli are a driving force in many of today's problems, including obesity, addiction to television and video games, and war," writes Deirdre Barrett, author of *Supernormal Stimuli*. "People sit alone in front of a plastic box streaming *Friends* instead of going out with their real buddies. They tend FarmVille crops while shirking their real duties. Men have sex with two-dimensional screen images when a willing partner may be in the next room."[2]

Few people would say this is really how they want to live. But this is

> **The deepest tragedy is that giving in to our desire for the fake distorts *us*. Psychologically. Sexually. Even physically.**

where we are. Real life, with its real risks and slower rhythms, struggles to compete with the short-term payoff we get from pixels.

None of us really want the kind of life that's spent relating to images instead of our actual wives. I love this bit from a Kurt Vonnegut novel, when one guy, Fred, hands another guy, Harry, a photo of a woman in a bikini.

> He nudged Harry, man-to-man.
> "Like that, Harry?" he asked.
> "Like what?"
> "The girl there."
> "That's not a girl. That's a piece of paper."[3]

Right! It's the ol' swindle again, and Harry knows it. That's not a woman at all. It's ink.

Or it's an arrangement of pixels on a screen. It's binary code. It's nothing, really.

Nothing at all.

Make no mistake, when we throw ourselves into nothingness, we'll end up feeling angry and meaningless. We shouldn't be surprised.

Video Games

I Love Them, and They're Just Too Awesome

No, seriously, I mean it. They're too awesome.

To make my point, let me tell you that back in the day, Atari made a "football" game. Honestly, the only way we knew it was a "football" game was because the label on the cartridge said "Football" and there was a drawing of football players on it.

The actual game bore no resemblance to the label or to football or to sports or to life on Earth. The "field" was vertical, and you could see all one hundred yards at once. The "ball" was square. It was one (1) giant pixel.

The playbooks encompassed two (2) whole plays. The "players" were just robots moving in unison, with an off-screen "crowd" making a strange grinding noise.

The Atari football game was primitive, repetitive, juvenile, pathetic, and ridiculous . . . and I played that thing for 4,506,201 hours.

And not because I was a kid either. I could still play it for hours in one sitting if given the chance. Long after everyone else has tapped out, I can keep playing video games.

This is why I stay away from immersive RPG-type hobbies. Not because role-playing games are inherently evil, but because they're simply too *fun* for me. I'm not kidding about this.

I call video games "awesome," and I use that word a lot. Of course, it means "super great" or "amazing" in the usual sense. But it's also from the word "awe," which means "inspiring fear or apprehension." When it comes to video games, I mean "awesome" in both senses.

I'm fearful of losing my life to these things.

My day-to-day, real life can't compete with gaming, which is another form of supernormal stimulation that can make me lose my taste for real things.

Real life is at a distinct disadvantage because it doesn't always seem to pay off. In games, I know if I collect enough whatever-points or kill all the villains on a particular level, I will level up. There's a fairly immediate win in games that doesn't always happen in reality.

I can have virtual adventures without any of the mundane work. If I pop in a military game, I skip right past all the real work of becoming a soldier. Suddenly, I'm a Navy SEAL without doing a single push-up or half-drowning in a freezing ocean during training. I can use advanced weaponry without ever learning a thing about them. How can reality compete?

> **My day-to-day, real life can't compete with gaming, which is another form of supernormal stimulation that can make me lose my taste for real things.**

For a lot of us, video games can make the rest of life pale and boring by comparison. Because they consistently provide a dopamine hit, our brains become hyper-reactive to it, and it can dull our appreciation of the rest of life.

Maybe we used to enjoy taking a long walk with our dog, but now we don't because we just want to get back to our game. The rest of life is just something to put up with until we can be with our precious game again. We become like Gollum in the cave with his ring. A friend of mine finally quit a strategy game he was playing when he realized he was thinking about it all the time, even while sitting in his law classes. He nearly failed the class before he thought, *You know, maybe this is a problem if this game is more important than law school.*

I just saw a photo of a thirty-four-year-old man named Ikuo. He's a normal-looking guy in a white T-shirt. The photo was taken in his room, which makes sense because Ikuo hadn't left his room in seven years. The photo was published on the National Geographic website as part of a story on a growing trend in Japan.

Known as hikikomori, these are people, mainly men, who haven't participated in society or shown a desire to do so for at least a year. They rely instead on their parents to take care of them. In 2016, the Japanese government census put the population of hikikomori at 540,000 for people aged fifteen to thirty-nine.[1] But it could easily be double that number. Since many prefer to stay entirely hidden, they remain uncounted.[2]

The hikikomori phenomenon isn't limited to Japan. People are increasingly shutting themselves out of real life and choosing to live their entire lives online. Please don't do this.

When I feel the pull to shut myself off from the world to play games, I wrestle with these questions:

If God created me, he had a purpose in mind. Was it for me to spend my days in unreality?

If the unnatural dopamine hits are altering my brain, rendering the rest of life bland and colorless in comparison to games, is that a problem?

If God created me to be the answer to others' problems and a blessing to the vulnerable, how tragic would it be if I was too busy playing some other character?

Now, I'm not giving you (or me) a no-games rule. That's not how this works. We have to go back to the big picture. The God of the Bible is unique. He's looking to go through life with you. There's a friendship aspect to this. He wants you and me to grow up so our desires will start to change. Then he can trust us to want the right things.

The hurting world and our hurting communities need us to solve real-world problems, protect real-world people, and fight real-world injustice. Please don't waste your God-given desire for adventure and accomplishment by being a fake hero fighting fake injustices in fake worlds. Join me in reality. It's not always the most exciting here. I've noticed that there are fewer explosions and I can't hop as high. Also, my first-person point of view is blurrier.

But when you take a deep breath and get over the dopamine addiction (and you can!), you'll see that the non-virtual reality is the reality you're perfect for.

Here's Some Good News about Pornography. No, Really.

So here's a chapter specifically about pornography, and I promise it's not a guilt trip. We already know we all have problems, and our culture seems precision-designed to mess up young guys. That's not my fault or yours. It's just where we are.

Here are a few things to think about, and then I'll get to the good news.

Pornography is truly a swindle. It attracts millions with the promise of sexiness . . . and then actually ruins sex for millions, causing even young men to have trouble being aroused by real women. Why? They simply can't relate to real women anymore. Porn exposure has literally made their brains different.[1]

Porn use means sexual problems for men. And that's fascinating because we again see how the fake can destroy the real, the true, and the beautiful.

Psychologist Philip Zimbardo wrote a book appropriately called *The Demise of Guys* in which he talks about "arousal addiction." Our brain is wired with "reward circuitry" for real life, the real world we live in, and real situations we find ourselves in. It's not made for the constant dopamine hits that come from pornography. This addiction is dangerous for all of us but particularly for young men, whose brains are still developing.[2]

Gary Wilson, in his TED Talk called "The Great Porn Experiment," talks about the mental health consequences of porn use. Arousal addiction symptoms are often mistaken for other things, like ADHD or social anxiety or concentration problems. Doctors will often prescribe medicine without asking about things like internet addictions. Wilson says (and this is important!), "Guys never realize they can overcome these symptoms simply by changing their behavior."[3]

Think about that. Wilson is saying that depression, ADHD, concentration problems . . . all are possibly (not always, of course, but perhaps often) linked to an addiction to arousal.

Porn works like any other addiction. It numbs our ability to get pleasure from simple day-to-day life. To get our dopamine hit, we've got to turn back to the only thing that will provide it.

But there's good news! Thankfully, a lot of people are finding that dramatic healing can happen pretty fast. Wilson quotes one man's experience giving up pornography:

> I've been to psychologists and psychiatrists for the last eight years. Have been diagnosed with depression, severe social anxiety, severe memory impairment, and a few others. Have tried Effexor, Ritalin, Xanax, Paxil. Dropped out of two different colleges, been fired twice, used pot to calm my social anxiety. I've been approached by quite a few women, I guess due to my looks and status, but they quickly flew away due to my incredible weirdness.
>
> I've been a hardcore porn addict since age 14. For the last two years, I've been experimenting and finally realized that porn was an issue. I stopped it completely two months ago. It's been very difficult, but so far, incredibly worth it. I've since quit my remaining medication. My anxiety is nonexistent. My memory and focus are sharper than they've ever been. . . . I seriously think I had a rebirth, a second chance at life.[4]

There's an online community at Reddit strictly about giving up porn, and more than 700,000 people belong to it. It's refreshing to read. The stories of what happens when guys get their minds away from porn are encouraging. One seventeen-year-old writes:

> I went from an introvert to an extrovert: not overnight, of course, but it was a slow process of getting more and more confidence to go out and not worry about talking to random strangers, and making new friends. . . . This has made life much, much easier for me.[5]

The following is from others on the Reddit forum:

> [On the benefits of going 284 days without porn.] I feel happier, more relaxed, less like I need a hit of dopamine. . . . I feel more in control of my life now.[6]

> I had serious anger issues [when using porn]. The two are DEFINITELY related. Watching porn changes our brain's chemical makeup so much that irritation, anger becomes a dominant emotion.[7]

> [After going 90 days without porn.] I can feel more emotions, I'm more confident. . . . I'm more motivated for school.[8]

More motivation! More in control! Less irritation! More confidence! This is all good news. So the question you might be asking is, "Okay, but how can I get better about eliminating porn from my life?"

Here's an extremely important thing (I think) we can do . . .

Get a Bigger Vision,
and Get Busy

Maybe you've already learned this, but if you want to give something up, something you've been addicted to, you must want something else *more*.

I had to learn this the hard way. Without a bigger vision for my life, I got caught up in a lot of harmful or just plain stupid and waste-of-time stuff.

This is true for all of us: *We need a bigger vision for our lives.* That bigger vision is everything.

I'm acting this out right now, as a matter of fact. I'm alone on my laptop, writing these words. Honestly, it's difficult and not immediately rewarding. I could open my internet browser and do something far easier. I could avail myself of some supernormal stimulation and get a momentary dopamine hit.

But . . . I'm not going to. Why? Because I want something else even more. I want a lot of things even more. Like these things, in no particular order:

1. I want my words to add value to your life. I can't do this if I don't focus.

2. I'd like to get this book done. My publisher would prefer that as well.

3. I don't want to be a hypocrite, writing one thing for you and doing another in my private life. I want to engage with God without an addiction (to porn or whatever) hovering over me.

4. I want to honor my wife. I want to be a man she is proud of. I want to desire my wife and enjoy a great sex life with a real woman, the one who, in turn, calls me out to be a man in all facets of my life.

5. I don't want to have a constant obstacle that makes me ashamed to talk to God.

6. I want to be a man who is fully present, ready to respond wisely and seeing things clearly.

7. I want to be energized. I want to be creative. I'm at my best when I have lots of ideas. I want to have a light heart. I don't want to be impatient and irritated by real life.

8. I don't want to look back in regret at all the things I didn't do that I could have. I don't want to waste my ambition on soul-killing stuff. I want to be able to think about far-off places and then, you know, go there.

9. I don't want to be numb. I want to be the Brant-iest Brant possible. I want to be fully human and have real human reactions, not dulled responses to beauty or transcendence. I don't want to go through life desensitized.

10. I'm not sure if I have a tenth thing, but it's weird to end a list on #9. (Maybe you can make up a tenth thing here: "I want_____." There. Now you get coauthor credit. Write your name next to mine on the cover.)

The bigger vision will win. Once we see it, we have to do whatever it takes to make the vision possible. It works this way with everything, really. Like exercise. I exercise every day, even though

I often don't feel like it. Why? Because I have a vision for my life that includes being healthy and looking and feeling a certain way.

I don't eat everything I want to eat. Why? Same reason. Donuts taste great, but if I had them every day for every meal, I wouldn't be as healthy or feel as good. I can say no to one thing in order to say yes to another.

We need to have a vision for our lives that is so much bigger than just being consumers of entertainment or super-normal stimuli.

We need to have a vision for our lives that is so much bigger than just being consumers of entertainment or supernormal stimuli.

Imagine being maximally you, instead of being dragged down into the muck of the surrounding culture. Sin deadens us.

It's God's desire that you live truly free. Not enslaved to foolish things that will only drag you down, but free to be the you we all need you to be.

A bigger vision will surely help. So will getting busy.

Here's what I mean. I used to take groups of high schoolers just over the border into Juarez, Mexico, to help build houses. We'd camp in tents outside the city. It was exhausting, sweltering work. Once, near the end of a trip, I asked some of the guys I'd long had a rapport with, "So . . . have you been struggling with lust this week?"

Lust had been their number one issue back home, but they suddenly realized they hadn't struggled with it much at all, even though it was a coed group. They said they hadn't had much time to think about it, and without media or the internet, it wasn't the usual constant battle.

They were just too busy.

Their minds were on other things. Their lives were structured differently. The work was hard, early morning to early evening. They were rarely alone. The work was full of laughs and making memories, and they could see the meaning in what they were accomplishing by helping a poor family have a decent shelter. Their minds were occupied by good things, and even in the short run, that made them different people.

Try it. Spend less time alone. Join groups or projects or causes. Get active. A wise man once told me, "Sometimes the key to moving past bad habits is simply changing your schedule," and it's true.

There's hope. Don't give up. Get a bigger vision, and get busy.

One More Short Chapter about Sex

Question the Culture

In the Bible, people of God are described as "foreigners and strangers" (Heb. 11:13). We don't fit easily into any culture. We'll always be at least a little weird to other people.

For example, in some cultures, the idea of loving our enemies sounds ridiculous. In our culture, the idea that sex should be between a man and a woman who are married to each other sounds bizarre to a lot of people.

Save sex for marriage? Find one woman? Commit yourself to her for the rest of your life? Take a vow in front of God and others that you will never, ever leave her? That's not exactly fashionable.

Our culture has chosen to reject God's wisdom in the area of sexuality. So, let's ask, Is this a good choice?

Think about it. What if everybody obeyed God in just this one particular area? How might life be different?

If we obeyed God in this one area, we'd probably be a lot healthier. Here are some numbers about sexually transmitted diseases: In just one year in the US alone, more than 1.5 million women are diagnosed with chlamydia. Another 700,000 people contract gonorrhea. Over 170,000 get syphilis.[1] About 1.2 million people in the US have HIV, which is predominantly spread through sexual contact.[2] Maybe God wanted us to avoid these diseases?

If we obeyed God in this one area, there wouldn't be widespread sexual abuse, harassment, and exploitation of women.

If we obeyed God in this one area, the US wouldn't have a record of more than forty million abortions.[3] There would be no tragic demand for abortions and no abortion industry required.

If we obeyed God in this one area, we wouldn't have a massive porn industry that preys on women and children. The porn industry makes more money than the NFL, NBA, and MLB combined.[4] Porn sites get more traffic than Amazon, X, and Netflix combined.[5]

Porn is also linked to violent behavior and abuse. It's cited in millions of divorce cases.[6] It forms addicts, even of children. And it's a huge driver behind human trafficking. Of course, if we obeyed God in just this one area, there would be no sex trafficking at all. There would be no sexual abuse of children.

If we obeyed God in this one area, there would be no broken families resulting from infidelity.

If we obeyed God in this one area, fatherlessness—one of the biggest contributors to imprisonment and poverty—would be largely erased.

And I'm just getting started. This topic could be a whole book by itself, but I don't want to get bogged down here. The point is this: When people act like God's wisdom is foolishness, *question the culture.*

Since God gives us freedom, we're free to royally muck things up. We're free to choose death instead of life.

Moses spelled out our freedom when he spoke to God's people thousands of years ago. As you read this, think about your own life ahead:

> Now listen! Today I am giving you a choice between life and death, between prosperity and disaster. For I command you this day to love the LORD your God and to keep his commands, decrees, and

regulations by walking in his ways. If you do this, you will live and multiply, and the LORD your God will bless you and the land you are about to enter and occupy.

But if your heart turns away and you refuse to listen, and if you are drawn away to serve and worship other gods, then I warn you now that you will certainly be destroyed. You will not live a long, good life in the land you are crossing the Jordan to occupy.

Today I have given you the choice between life and death, between blessings and curses. Now I call on heaven and earth to witness the choice you make. Oh, that you would choose life, so that you and your descendants might live! You can make this choice by loving the LORD your God, obeying him, and committing yourself firmly to him. This is the key to your life. (Deut. 30:15–20 NLT)

You have the freedom to pursue wisdom or foolishness. You have the freedom to become the young man we need you to be or to waste your life. You have the freedom to embrace the real over the fake, to choose connection over disconnection.

Life or death.

Blessings or curses.

Choose wisely.

PROTECT
THE VULNERABLE

Your Neighborhood Should Be Safer Simply Because You're There

Let me tell you about Dishal Sooku. He's a quiet guy. He works hard. He likes to laugh.

One day he was sitting at a table with his dad. They were on a veranda outside the small restaurant Dishal owns in South Africa. He noticed two women and a small child, a girl. His dad noticed a "suspicious-looking guy" nearby and told Dishal to keep an eye on him.

That's when the guy jumped a short railing and lunged to kidnap the little girl. Little did he know that he had no chance.

Almost instantaneously—it's on video, you can watch it—Dishal is on top of the guy, throwing him to the ground and putting him in a choke hold.

"I saw the video again and I thought, 'How did I do that?'" Dishal said. "All those thoughts go through your mind. But I guess, at that moment, when I saw the little girl, everything else just took over."[1]

Dishal had years of martial arts experience. He needed it all for that one moment. He said he surprised himself that he acted so fast. He held the attacker until the police came, and the attacker was charged with attempted kidnapping.

"A big part of martial arts is that you learn to control the situation, and I think that is what happened," Dishal said. "I needed to control him so that he would let go of this child. It was a combination of awareness and training and all that."[2]

I love this guy's story for a few reasons:

1. It went viral worldwide. People hunger for stories where someone steps in to defend the vulnerable.
2. Because Dishal trained for years, he was able to do something he wouldn't have been able to do otherwise. Self-discipline makes us capable of remarkable things.
3. He credits not just his training but his and his dad's awareness. They were actively looking out for the people around them.
4. And my favorite aspect: Dishal Sooku is unassuming. Little did the women with the girl know that they were safer because of a quiet man at a table nearby.

The people in your neighborhood, at your school, or at your workplace should be safer because you're there.

Simply because you're in the mix, they're better off. If the world around you is your garden and you're going to be faithful to keep it, then kids, older folks, and other vulnerable people around you are safer.

The people in your neighborhood, at your school, or at your workplace should be safer because you're there.

Most of them won't be aware of it, but that's okay. In fact, they may suspect the opposite. People often consider young men something of a threat, and that's understandable.

A full 80 percent of violent crimes in the US are committed by men, and men are at their highest likelihood of committing a violent crime before age twenty-five.[3]

Young men are in their athletic, physical prime before age twenty-five. It's also true that before that age, their brains haven't fully developed.[4] They're much more likely to take risks. They're given a desire for adventure and a desire to push the envelope.

This desire isn't a bad thing in and of itself. In fact, it's a good thing. It's to help you as a young man rise to the challenge of leaving your comfortable home. It's to give you the drive to set out on your own, take responsibility for your own life and livelihood, and start your own family someday.

It's not there to prompt you to drive 140 miles per hour on the interstate and jeopardize people's lives.

So use your God-given drive to do something good. Use it to defend people, not threaten them.

The other morning in my neighborhood, I walked by a little girl with a backpack. She was coming my way on the sidewalk, and she quickly zipped by without making eye contact.

In a different era, maybe, I would've smiled and said hello. But I know it's likely she was taught not to engage with strangers, particularly strange men. I know this because I told my daughter the very same thing. It makes sense.

But you know what? This girl is actually safer because I'm around, even if she doesn't know it. I will look out for her. When I've seen suspicious or abusive activity in our neighborhoods, I've physically intervened to defend the kids. Would I get pummeled in a street fight? Maybe. But that's okay.

Even if you're like me and not physically intimidating, speaking up can be very effective. It's remarkable how quickly some people will back down when someone—anyone at all—challenges them.

We've been placed where we are for a reason, and it's not to assault or threaten. It's to protect. Like Dishal, we should make it a habit to take note of what's happening around us. We should notice if someone's behaving strangely and be ready to intervene on behalf of others.

I don't want to be passive. I want to watch over people and use whatever I have to defend them. We can all do this with our applied intelligence, our words, our bodies, our money, and our lives.

Whether people notice or praise us isn't the issue. We know that our Creator sees us doing exactly what he created us to do.

If the men show up, the most vulnerable aren't so vulnerable anymore.

They have us.

What You Do Actually *Matters*

Maybe you've wondered, *If God can do anything he wants, why does he need me to do anything? If there are people to feed or protect or rescue or whatever, why doesn't he do it himself?*

Fair questions! And here's my response: God doesn't *need* us for anything. He needs nothing. But what he *wants* is our partnership. He wants us to experience playing an important role in his kingdom.

Remember this: There are some things that won't get done if you don't do them. There are some things for which you are Plan A and there is no Plan B.

This means that what you do actually *matters*. What you say matters. What you do with your money matters. Whether you defend the vulnerable matters. When you fail, well, that matters too. You can't just say, "If God wants it done, he'll do it."

When we want to start the car in the morning, we don't say, "Well, if God wants me to get to work, *he* will start the car." No, because we have the keys. And most of us have hands and wrists. We can put the key in the ignition like so, and *bam*—the car starts.

A few weeks ago in our town, a middle school girl was in a minivan that was struck by a motorcyclist going 120 miles per hour. She was killed. I believe that if the young man on the motorcycle had not made the choice to drive recklessly, she would still be alive. The evil and foolish things we do matter too.

There was another recent incident here in which a woman accidentally drove her car into a canal. The car was sinking. She had almost drowned when a police officer jumped in and pulled her to safety. I believe that if he hadn't done that, she would be dead.

A few years ago, a man with an AK-47 intended to kill everyone on a train in France. The death toll, according to the investigators, would likely have been three hundred people. The man had planned everything and brought enough ammunition to kill every man, woman, and child on board. But among the passengers were three young men who decided to intervene physically. They took him down and subdued him until the authorities arrived.

If you don't do something, don't just assume it will get done. Your life is deeply meaningful, one way or another. You're the only one uniquely placed in your position in the world.

Did it really matter that they acted? Of course it did! But most people on the train wouldn't have made that choice. That's probably why the young men's actions resulted in tears of relief and gratitude, France's highest honor, and a Clint Eastwood movie.

If you don't do something, don't just assume it will get done. Your life is deeply meaningful, one way or another. You're the only one uniquely placed in your position in the world. No one else is in your exact context.

━━ ━━ ━━ ━━

Once, I was riding in a van in a city in Senegal, Africa. Senegal is a very hot, dry place, and it was extraordinarily hot on this particular day. The streets were jammed with people shopping and selling in the heat and exhaust of the intense traffic.

As we sat at a stoplight, I saw a tall, relatively young woman in a vivid blue dress gesturing to us. She was carrying a bag of nuts and clearly was hoping we'd buy some. She looked distressed.

I tried to avoid eye contact with her, and the van soon set off when the light turned green. We moved forward and stopped at the light a block farther. I looked back . . . and saw the woman in the blue dress behind us, now running to catch up to us. She was dodging and weaving between all the people on the street. It was over one hundred degrees, and in the intense sunshine and through the filth of the street, she was sprinting in her long blue dress.

She had the look of true desperation. I wondered why she was so motivated to catch up to us, then it popped into my head: She had children she was determined to feed. She'd seen foreigners in a van, and foreigners usually had money. Someone might buy her peanuts!

The van pulled forward, and I looked back again. She was still running. I asked the driver to pull over, and he did. The young woman finally caught up with us. The heat rolled into the van as we lowered a window.

"I'll buy some peanuts," I said. She indicated that they cost a dollar, so I handed a dollar to the person by the window. None of the other Americans in the van were interested. They weren't hungry, they said. And our van pulled away.

I watched the woman turn away and begin walking back.

I tell you this story even though I'm not sure there's anything remarkable about it. It's just one of those memories that sticks in my head, and every time I think about it, I feel something like a punch in the stomach. You know why? Regret.

I had more cash. I gave her one lousy dollar.

She didn't make me feel guilty. She didn't ask for more. It's just that I could have given her fifty dollars, or whatever I had, and it wouldn't have hurt me in the slightest. I meet a desperate woman, and give her . . . *one dollar*? This was a small moment, a quick decision for me, but it could have been incredibly significant for her.

I know God forgives me for things. But I also know that what we do has consequences. What we do actually matters. We have real opportunities, and we can seize them and bring real mercy into people's lives.

Or not.

But oh, how it matters.

The Ultimate Betrayal

If I'm right (and I totally am) that true masculinity is rooted in our unique role as keepers of our personal gardens and that we're called to protect and defend and help the vulnerable, then there's a flip side. *Becoming* a threat to those vulnerable people . . . is treason.

And so is being passive in the presence of threats to them.

As I write this, there's a story in the news about Olivia, an eight-year-old, and her little brother, RJ, who's four. They went for their first ever sledding outing and lost control. Their mom and dad could see it happening from atop a hill, but they couldn't do anything about it. The sled was going too fast, picking up momentum.

And then it steered straight into an icy pond.

The parents saw a fourteen-year-old boy named Kieren Foley jump into the water. He grabbed little RJ first and handed him to a friend who had also jumped into the water. And then RJ was handed to another teenage boy . . . and another . . . and another . . . until he was safe.

Five teenage guys had jumped into the freezing water and quickly made a human chain to rescue both RJ and Olivia.

"We definitely had to do something. We can't just sit there and watch," Kieren said.

"We hope that anybody would do that," said Tyler Armagan. "It just happened to be us there."

"What they did was, like, just amazing," RJ and Olivia's dad said. "It was awesome to see little kids do that."[1]

In this situation, it was obvious there was no halfway. Either the guys got in the water or they didn't.

In our daily lives, the right action may not be so obvious. We may never be recognized as heroes for doing the right thing or using our lives to make people more secure. If we live our lives just to serve ourselves, no one may ever call us out on it.

Many people may not see it, but heroism is quite real, and so is treason. In another chapter, we'll discuss in more detail making women feel secure, but for now let's talk about the opposite: making women feel insecure.

For the women who know you—whether it's a sister, mother, neighbor, coworker, whoever—it should be unthinkable that you would harm them. And for the women who don't know you yet, you have to interact with them knowing that even your physical stature or strength can represent a threat. Women around the world and for centuries have often been at the mercy of the men around them. It's no mystery why they can feel menaced by male behavior that's even subtly scary.

For the women who know you—whether it's a sister, mother, neighbor, coworker, whoever—it should be unthinkable that you would harm them.

If you get married, remember this: If you are passive like Adam, flirt with other women, have an explosive temper, or have a way of making your wife feel like you don't care about her . . . that's a betrayal of your role.

Think about it. If you do get married, you'll be making a vow to a woman. She'll be pinning her hopes on you. Whether she says it or not, she'll be hoping you'll be a keeper of the garden, someone who can rise to the occasion and be a defender of the weak. She'll be betting her future on you.

Are you going to be a threat to her? Will you make her feel insecure instead of adding to her security? Instead of cheering her on and promoting her and helping her take on the world, will you undermine her? No. That can't happen. You cannot become the enemy in the garden. That's like being the curator of an important historical museum, being trained and trusted to guard precious artifacts, and then smashing them on the floor.

The culture we are in seems designed to get us to betray our role. It seems to set us up to see women as objects to exploit or to see a commitment to our own children as optional. It wants us to be consumers of entertainment, and that's it. It wants us to stay little boys.

I say this as a grown man: There aren't many of us out here. We need you.

If you decide to be a keeper of the garden, a creator of order, peace, and security, you will stand out like . . . like . . . what's the phrase?

Oh, yes—a man among boys.

The Most Vulnerable Person
I've Ever Met

Years ago, I was emceeing a concert by artist Toby Mac. I am a terrible emcee, but since I'm on the radio, people keep asking me to do it.

I was asked to mention "cure" from the stage as part of the announcements. But I didn't know what "cure" was, so I had to ask. A woman with CURE (they capitalize it) told me it's a network of hospitals that provides surgeries for the most vulnerable children in the world—kids with disabilities in developing nations.

These are kids whose problems could have been fixed quickly had they been born in the US, but where they live, their disabilities dominate their lives. They're considered cursed and often wind up defenseless and abused.

The patients and their desperate families are used to being treated as freaks and outcasts, but CURE hospitals are dedicated to flipping that upside down and letting them know about a God who loves them. These children aren't cursed. They matter deeply. They are not forgotten. In fact, God draws close to them.

I told the CURE staff that I'd love to see a hospital in action. They said, "Want to come to Afghanistan?"

Uh . . . sure?

Months later, I arrived at the hospital, completely disoriented. The smell of gasoline and exhaust throughout Kabul, the sight of women in burqas bringing their children into the waiting area, the sound of many languages, and then a further disorienting question from the nursing staff: "Would you like to do kangaroo duty?"

"Uh . . . yes? I mean, I haven't spent much time in hospitals. Does this involve hopping?"

The staff had me wash up and took me to a neonatal intensive care unit. I sat down in a rocking chair. They had me unbutton a couple top buttons of my shirt. Then they handed me a person.

A very, very, very small person.

A one-pound person.

They said her family name was Zakara—she hadn't been given a first name yet, since her family didn't expect her to make it. And could I please hold her? She had been very sick, but she needed to make skin contact with someone.

So that's kangaroo duty, apparently. I sat there, holding this tiniest of persons to my chest. I didn't know humans could be this small. She would grab my finger and look up at me. She wanted to make eye contact.

People in the room eventually filed out until it was just this tiny girl and me. I could feel her little breaths, and it just seemed impossible that someone this small could exist.

I had just landed in Afghanistan, and now it was she and I.

We rocked for an hour or two. It was long enough for me to do a lot of thinking.

I thought about her and how she might be one of the world's biggest underdogs. She was from a poor family. She was in war-torn Afghanistan. As a girl, she had second-class status and few protections from abuse. At this point, she was nameless.

She was a scrap of life. A little scrap of life with nearly translucent skin. She was too tiny to be real, but here she was. She was looking up at me. I was looking down at her.

If the kingdom of God as described in the Bible is a real thing, this "scrap of life"? She's royalty!

What prestige does she have? None. What status? None. What wealth? Zero. What has she accomplished? Absolutely nothing. But in God's economy, the first are last and the last are first.

You know what? I like that. A lot.

I like underdogs. Maybe you do too. I like a God who champions them. I like a God who turns our messed-up values system on its head. He is a defender of widows, orphans, the poor, and tiny people like that little girl.

I sat with her and rocked and thought about what kind of man I want to be. I decided I too want to be a defender of widows, orphans, the poor, and tiny people like that little girl.

———

I've since met hundreds of other patients at CURE hospitals around the world. This has been my work and the focus of my giving in both energy and money for years. I've gotten to play a role in the healing of thousands of kids with correctible disabilities.

I'm telling you this because I'm so deeply thankful I get to be a part of it.

I'm also telling you this because I want you to think about how *you* might be a protector of the vulnerable no matter who you are or where you're from, using whatever gifts you have.

I'm not a surgeon. I'm not a firefighter. I'm not a military guy. I'm not rich. I'm from a tiny town in Illinois. I'm on the autism spectrum. I'm from a broken home. But I use whatever gifts I have to bring mercy to children and their desperate families, and I can't stop being thankful for it and energized by it.

You and I don't have to fit the stereotypes of what manly men look or sound like. What we do need to do is use whatever we have as great keepers of the garden to defend the defenseless.

You can do this even if you're working the most seemingly meaningless job. You can give to an organization that accomplishes your mission (it certainly doesn't have to be CURE; there are a lot of great ones), and instantly—*bam*—your work takes on more meaning. You're not just detailing cars, for instance; you're using your hard work to help heal a teenage girl in Malawi who's never walked before. And all the people around her will see her go from crying to dancing. They'll see an advance trailer of heaven.

Speaking of heaven, maybe that girl and her crying-with-joy family will get to thank you personally someday.

That car-detailing job is an important one, right? Now you're a rescuer.

Planning for the Future

What "Home" Looks Like

If your current family is a mess, I have some good news: If or when you start your own family, it can be different. And not just a little different. It can be totally different. Totally *better*.

When I was growing up, my home felt unstable and scary. I remember feeling afraid of my dad. He was (and still is) bigger than me, and his behavior seemed bizarre, erratic, and threatening to me. Despite my mom's best efforts, home was a frightening place for me to be. When I walked home from school and saw his car parked outside, I didn't want to go in.

When my parents were first divorced, I felt safer. But then they remarried, hoping to keep the family together, before getting divorced again.

I remember one night when I was twelve or so saying to myself, "If I ever have a family of my own, I know what kind of dad I'm *not* going to be."

And you know what? I'm not that kind of dad.

When my own kids were growing up, our home had a completely different atmosphere. It provided security. My wife, Carolyn, and I had clear expectations for behavior, and our home was warm and fun. My kids are in their twenties now, and they have no memories of a childhood like I had. None. My wife and kids always felt protected. As a kid, I decided that if I had anything to say about it, my future family would have laughter and warmth and consistency and yet more laughter in our home, and that's what it was like.

I want you to know you can live a different life. If you have a dad who is a massive disappointment, you are not doomed to become like him. Not at all. You can set an entirely different tone in your own home. If you are always gentle and respectful with your wife and kids, your family will tend toward gentleness with and respect for each other.

If you end up being away too often or you're passive and disengaged, chaos can sweep in. Human nature can take over, like weeds choking out the garden you're supposed to keep.

You don't have to be perfect. I certainly wasn't. But if you can be home and plugged-in and take time to truly enjoy your wife and kids, well . . . it doesn't get much better than that. Your kids will grow up knowing you and loving you.

You set the tone.

It's remarkable how this plays out in sports. Almost instantly, a new coach can radically impact a team's performance, and not just from an X's-and-O's standpoint. The entire atmosphere of the team can change from ragged and undisciplined to streamlined, peaceful, and effective, simply as a result of the demeanor of the team's leadership and what that leadership values.

This is the effect you can have. It's almost magical. If you're at peace, growing as a believer, and active, present, and engaged, your home will be peaceful. Everyone will benefit.

The world is chaotic. It's judgmental and disordered and, sadly, even physically threatening. Homes should be a getaway where peace rules and the vulnerable are protected, not threatened.

If you're a young man still living with your original family, you can start protecting the vulnerable people in your home now. Your mother is vulnerable even if she's highly accomplished, confident, and strong. Same with your dad. They're not as strong as you may think. People rarely are. You have weapons that can hurt them, even if it's just your words.

Take care to show mercy now. There's no reason to wait. To the extent that you can, demonstrate kindness toward your parents and your (possibly annoying) siblings. Not only is it the right thing to do, not only will it start shaping you into a man who takes responsibility, but it will also probably kind of freak people out (in a good way). So it's a win-win-win!

If you're a young man still living with your original family, you can start protecting the vulnerable people in your home now.

Remember, God created a garden and humans to inhabit it. He told the humans to go forth and multiply. He wanted to see, and still wants to see, the whole world become more like Eden, a place where peace rules. It's the kind of peace that lets little things grow and flourish and blossom.

That's what a home truly must be like. It's your garden. Remember that even if your current home is in chaos, your next one doesn't need to be.

Thank God.

BE AMBITIOUS ABOUT THE RIGHT THINGS

Reality Is What Hits You
When You're Wrong

You know how you think of just the right thing to say only after you had the chance to say it?

I had the opposite happen for the first time the other day. I actually said the right thing right on time, and it was super cool. I felt suave.

I had a short Uber ride to a restaurant. The driver was a very outgoing, middle-aged guy from New York. Somehow, we got into a deep conversation within about a minute. We talked about forgiveness and anger and recognizing our own ability to justify whatever we want. I loved talking with him.

As he dropped me off, I opened the back door and started to get out. He said, "Hey, wait a second. Just curious what you think about this. Can we even really know what reality is? I mean, what if we're just imagining things? That's my question. I mean, what is reality?"

Pretty deep question. I stood there with the door open, ducking just enough to look at him.

"Reality," I said, "is what hits you when you're wrong."

He paused and then laughed. "Wow . . . that's so true. Wow. Thanks, man!"

I nodded with a super-cool knowing smile, waved, shut the door, and walked off like . . . well, like super-cool guys who say cool stuff walk off in the movies.

This seriously happened. I'm going to remember it forever because it was so completely drop-the-mic-y. I'll also remember it forever because it will never, ever happen again.

The thing is, I'd just heard Dallas Willard say those words in a podcast an hour before. So there's that. I didn't feel like I had time to attribute, but if you're reading this, Uber guy, please know I totally stole that from Dallas Willard.

— — — —

Here's an even less inspiring story. Years ago, I forgot my keys.

Now, it's also true that I forgot my keys today. And yesterday. But this particular forgetting-of-the-keys took place after an event in a large church building with a long hallway.

When I realized I'd forgotten my keys, I remembered they were upstairs in the kitchen. I was proud of myself for remembering. I quickly walked down the long, dimly lit hallway, saw a skinny post right in the middle, and walked to the left of it. No problem.

I went up the stairs, found my keys, and jogged back down. I picked up speed and started flat-out running. I saw the post. I did not hit the post. That would be silly. Instead, I once again moved to the left of it, this time at full speed.

I smashed into a glass wall. With my face. While I was sprinting.

The glass wall had wire mesh in it, so it shattered where my head bashed into it. It also shattered where my knee bashed into it. And also where my hand punched it.

Somehow, I stayed sort of conscious. I just bounced off the glass and stood there. Some people came running, wondering what the *boom* was in the hallway. They found me dazed. And bleeding a lot. They told me later that I'd said, "I'm so sorry, I think I broke a wall." Then they hustled me off to the emergency room.

I tell you this ridiculous story because I want you to know that we don't construct reality. Reality did not bend to my beliefs. I physically bounced off reality.

Reality was what hit me when I was, you know . . . wrong.

Yes, I was intellectually convinced that there was nothing in the way of my path. That's why I was running. I was truly sincere in my belief. I was 100 percent committed. What I wanted—to simply run to the front door—was very innocent and would hurt no one. But what I wanted didn't change reality.

My sincerity does not change reality.

Jesus talks about the kingdom of God as the deepest reality. It's worth trading everything else for. It's worth more than all the power or prestige or money we can have in the moment. Because it's lasting and it recognizes the true King, it's more real than anything else.

Jesus said if we put his words into practice, we're like someone who builds a house on a rock. When storms hit, the place is fine. But if we don't put Jesus' words into practice, we're like someone who builds a house on sand. When storms hit, it's game over.

Was the one who built their house on sand convinced it would last? Of course. Otherwise, why make the investment of time and energy? But the house collapsed anyway, because reality is what hits you when . . . you know.

If you are ambitious about the wrong things, you will be hit by reality, good and hard. I talked to a friend just this morning who wishes he could go back to the time when his kids were young, get his priorities straight, and value time with them more than work. But he can't.

If you are ambitious about the wrong things, you will be hit by reality, good and hard.

The key is to ask for wisdom. Wisdom means knowing what matters and what doesn't, or what matters more and what matters less. You don't want to go through life without it. It's the difference between a life of meaning and one of meaninglessness.

We should talk about that, so . . .

If You Feel Meaninglessness, It Might Be Because You're Investing Time and Energy in Meaningless Things

Mark this down: You will struggle with feeling meaningless when you choose to invest your time and energy in meaningless things.

I know this from personal experience. Lots of personal experience.

By the way, I'm not talking about your work or school. Those things are not meaningless. As we'll discuss shortly, even if your job or studies seem trivial, they're not. They matter to others, they matter to God, and they should matter very much to you.

What I'm talking about are things that don't add value to anyone's life. We are created to add value to things. When we are at our best, that's exactly what we're doing. We're making things, we're changing things, we're improving conditions and situations for the people around us—those for whom we take responsibility.

It's as sure as gravity. If I'm engaged only in activities and projects that ultimately yield nothing, I will feel it.

If I want to play video games all day, I can. And you know what? I'll enjoy it while I'm doing it. But there will be a psychological price to pay at the end of that day.

Over the course of time, if I'm spending significant time entertaining myself, I'll begin to feel ennui, which is a perfect word because (1) it's French, so I can say it with a pretentious accent and people think I'm cultured, and (2) it means listlessness and dissatisfaction that comes from not being occupied with anything that matters.

If you are not mission focused, you will feel ennui. Millions of men do, and I've certainly felt it. But I'm telling you, it's directly related to what I'm watching and doing and where I'm putting my attention.

It's tough to exist in our culture and not deal with ennui. This is partly due to our affluence. We tend not to struggle for food or shelter anymore. Most of us don't wake up with a start, thinking, *I've got to hunt or we'll starve soon.*

I don't want to live that way, though I have to admit, ennui would not be an issue. But that's the way most humans lived for thousands of years. They were a part of communities, villages, and tribes that were motivated to work together for survival. Survival was always the big issue. But now? The biggest issue may be what entertainment to choose next.

I know now that my mission is to be a keeper of the garden. I'm here to protect the vulnerable, care for the sick, and be a voice of peace in this anxious world. I'm here to make people feel secure and safe. I'm here to re-create and add beauty and cultivate and defend and, hopefully, add value to others' lives.

Honestly, the last two days are a perfect example of me *not* doing that. I've been putting off writing. (I heard someone say, "A real writer is someone who spends their time avoiding writing," so I totally qualify, at least on that level.) Yesterday I did the basic stuff: taking care of the dog, getting some batteries and things at the store. And I played lots of *EA Sports FC* on the PlayStation. Lots. Way too much. I did very little meaningful work. All *EA Sports FC*.

At the end of the day, I was listless. Surprise!

Today I got up early and forced myself to write this. I'm thinking of you as I type. I honestly want you to know how important it is to be mission driven. I don't want you to become like so many other men who are lifeless shells of who they should be and who we need them to be.

And I'm feeling way less listless. I'm even energized. I'm doing my thing, and I'm motivated by wanting to serve you. I'm also motivated by this: If you take the approach to manhood I've shared in this book, the women and children and men around you will be the beneficiaries.

I've noticed that people who are actively serving others don't struggle with feeling meaningless. It's a lesson I keep learning. My life isn't a highlight reel or social media feed. It's how I actually spend my days. If I fill my days with purpose, I tend to be less tired and invigorated. If I don't, I start questioning everything and grow more depressed.

I've noticed that people who are actively serving others don't struggle with feeling meaningless.

If you pay attention to things that help you keep the garden around you, you'll absolutely feel less ennui. I promise.

You're not created for entertainment alone. You'll really come alive when you're adding value to others' lives.

Invest in meaningless things and you'll yield meaninglessness. You'll also yield a vague, low-lying-but-quite-real anger at yourself. You may not be able to pin down why you're feeling this way, but the anger is there. It will come out in all sorts of ways. You'll be easily aggravated and less patient. You'll be more judgmental of the people you don't like and more prone to jealousy and bitterness.

Everything we choose to pay attention to is ultimately life-giving or ennui-giving.

This isn't to say never watch a movie or play a game. It's just that the fun thing is often the easy thing, and over time it becomes a trap. We wind up off mission and frustrated at ourselves and the world, our energy drained from us. We don't have to wonder why.

We also wind up very, very boring. Be ready for that too.

Right now, I'm energized. It's because I made myself do my thing. Funny how that works.

Women Care about This A Lot, Just FYI

In a sense, this whole book is about being ambitious for the right things. But here's an advance warning: People rarely applaud for the right things. You may not get much immediate feedback at all.

Do something dumb or selfish and you can win fans. Do something self-controlled and honorable and it's entirely likely no one will notice. The strength of humility is not often celebrated.

If, say, you offer consistent extreme takes on X, you can build a fan base. Echo someone's anger and they will quickly retweet you. You'll make some enemies, but you can also get positive feedback from your tribe. It's an ego stroke, and we tend to gravitate to where our egos are stroked.

Few people will cheer you for being self-controlled. You'll likely never get a comment praising you for not responding. You'll never get an Instagram comment that says, "Way to help people behind the scenes without us knowing about it!"

Most praiseworthy things don't get praised, so it can be hard to stay focused. But what you're ambitious about makes all the difference.

If you get married, your wife will need you to be ambitious. By "ambitious," I don't mean being an influencer or CEO, buying a big house, or going in the first round of the NBA draft, although there's nothing inherently wrong with any of these things. I mean simply that she'll respect you when she sees you have a drive to get things done. Productive things. Keeper-of-the-garden things. She'll need you to have a drive to do what's right and a motivation to protect her and your family.

She'll be impressed when you do things in real life. You know, non-video-game things. Even scoring personal records on *Call of Duty* are not as attractive as actually doing real things. (Ask me how I know this.)

This is not just about making money. I know two guys whose wives make a lot of money, and both of these men stay home and don't have jobs. One is very respected by his wife, and the other one isn't.

The first one attacks his responsibilities. He takes care of his wife and supervises the education of their daughters. He works on myriad projects. He doesn't tend to waste time. He gets things done for other people. He's a leader. He remains ambitious.

The other does pretty much nothing. Not only does his wife not respect him, I'm pretty sure no one does.

Look, your wife will *want* to respect you, but she won't be able to if you aren't actively making her and her home more secure.

Your wife may make more money than you. That could be threatening, but you don't need to be threatened *if* you remain engaged and forward-moving about things that have deep value. Maybe she makes good money working at a bank, and you make much less while running a Boys & Girls Club for at-risk kids or while working as a police officer. She'll still respect you if you're driven to accomplish things that matter and work with determination and passion.

If you become lazy, apathetic, or unwilling to work hard for the family or others, she'll sense that you're not fulfilling your mission. And she'll be right.

Do not underrate this factor in women's attraction to men. In fact, to most women, a man with enthusiastic purpose who isn't rich is far more attractive than a lazy, purposeless man who happens to have money. Ask them.

However, disordered ambition is destructive. Working eighteen-hour days to buy a high-end motorcycle is sort of ambitious, but it may not make a wife feel more secure.

Here's another example. When my wife, Carolyn, and I were first married, I was a lead singer in a rock band. We were pretty good, although, in the precise words of one record company executive, I had "the stage presence of a sponge on a stick." (I'm not making that up. I still laugh about it.)

To most women, a man with enthusiastic purpose who isn't rich is far more attractive than a lazy, purposeless man who happens to have money.

We practiced once or twice a week and played gigs every few weeks or so. Sometimes we'd play late nights in restaurants and bars and sometimes at music festivals or for church youth groups. The band seemed to be taking off.

But Carolyn was agitated with me. I really couldn't understand why. I wasn't gone that much, the guys I was playing with were good guys, and I never flirted with girls at gigs or anything.

It took me a while to get it. She was unsettled that the band might become my main thing. We hadn't been married long enough for her to know conclusively that I wouldn't let that happen. The band was a threat to her.

Now that we've been married for decades, she'd be fine with me playing in a band. (Please play with me in a band. Thanks. Wait, what's that? You want to name the band Sponge on a Stick? YOU ARE A GENIUS.) If I had, in fact, begun traveling extensively in hopes of being some kind of rock star, leaving my wife behind, it would have been ambition of a kind, certainly. But it would have been disordered ambition, pulling me toward applause and distracting me from my role as keeper of the garden. I'd be hurting my wife.

Rightly ordered ambition is a very good thing. And should you get married, these are the big questions you'll need to ask yourself:

Am I making my wife feel more secure?

Do my actions indicate that I'm willing to do what it takes to be here for her and for our kids?

Does she sense that I'm engaged with real life, ready to do what might need to be done for her?

In the garden I'm to watch over, my wife is the most beautiful flower. I want her to bloom, and rightly placed ambition will give her room to flourish.

A Quick Word

How to Be Incredibly Awesome and Somehow Less Attractive to Women

It's true: Women think risky guys are attractive!

Until they think they're stupid.

At first, if you're a risky, "dangerous" guy, you have a quality about you that seems promising. Maybe you aspire to be a BASE-jumping superstar or an awesome cliff diver, or you want to run with the bulls in Pamplona. It's all very cool.

Until it's not.

So when does this risk-taking make the jump from wildly attractive to stupid? When a woman trusts you with her future. When she needs you. And if you have a kid, this unnecessary risk-taking goes from being highly attractive to the exact opposite. You're actually *less* attractive to her if you're taking dumb risks.

This is because the original attraction was based on who she thought you *might* be: someone who will do what it takes to defend and provide for those around you. Your seeming bravery suggests to her that you're likely to rise to the occasion to fend off threats and ensure long-term stability.

But let's say you get married and your wife is taking care of three little kids while you're risking life and limb purely for the rush of it. You may find she doesn't think your hobby makes you hot anymore. "But you used to think it was hot," you might say. "You used to like it. You've changed, not me."

Unwittingly, you've revealed the problem. You haven't changed, but you needed to. You needed to go from Seems-Like-He'll-Be-a-Good-Provider-and-Protector Guy to Actual-Good-Provider-and-Protector Guy.

Your cool hobby has now become a threat to your wife's long-term security.

As a married father, I've taken some risks. For example, I've been to Afghanistan multiple times, staying in Kabul neighborhoods, and each time was a significant risk. The only reason my wife was proud of me rather than disgusted was because the trips were for a purpose. I used my given platform, applying whatever skills I have, to highlight the work of the CURE hospital that served Afghan women and children.

Each time, my wife and I had to talk at length, weigh out whether the trip was worth it, and arrive at a decision together. We both realized that while the trips were somewhat dangerous, they were to protect and defend the vulnerable.

Do I kind of enjoy the excitement of a unique, on-the-edge experience? Yes. There's something to that. But if it's just for my experience, well, that wouldn't fly with the mother of my children, nor should it.

I read a story about a young man who wanted to be a YouTube star. He got someone to film him as he stood at the top of the Pennybacker Bridge in Austin, Texas, and then jumped into the Colorado River. Someone watching him do it called 911, and he was rescued after fracturing his skull.

His comment later: "You might see it as jumping for views. I see more. . . . I don't settle for less. I will leave my mark on this planet."[1]

Okay. But do you really want to leave it with your skull?

Was the jump dangerous? Yes. Was it attractive to women? Probably not. Why? There was no point other than ego.

Purposeless, just-for-the-rush risk? Grow out of it.

Risks in the defense of others? Oh yes, you're made for that.

It's really not complex. I'm sure you got the point when I started this chapter, but I thought I'd keep going because I just love this point so much.

Run through fire to prove you're a man? You're not a man.

Run through fire to save a baby? Now you're talking.

Ambition and Work

Even Terrible Jobs Are Great

Now, let's talk about your job. It's awesome. That's right, even if it's terrible.

Even terrible jobs make us serve people. In fact, that's what you're being paid to do—serve people. And not just your bosses either.

This is obvious if you're a server at a restaurant. But it's also true of practically every single job you can imagine. You're being paid to be a help to people.

If you're stocking shelves at a grocery store, you're helping busy moms and dads gather the food they need for their families.

If you're doing tough lawn work, you're likely helping a lot of people who aren't physically able to do it themselves.

If you're flipping burgers, you're preparing someone's meal. Maybe a grandma. Maybe a little kid. Whoever it is you're feeding, that someone is incredibly important to God.

Would you be doing any of those things if you didn't get paid? Probably not. But that doesn't diminish the reality that you're serving people and that your efforts are adding value to their lives. That's a very healthy thing.

There's a famous story of two men in late middle age at a construction site. When asked, "What are you doing?" the first man says, "I'm stacking some blocks on top of each other." The second one, who's doing the exact same task, says, "I'm building a marvelous cathedral that will stand for centuries and inspire all who see it."

Yes, you can say, "I'm making a stupid ice cream cone at McDonald's." Or you can view it as fashioning something delightful, and even a little merciful, for a seven-year-old boy who just had an embarrassing day on a baseball field.

You can say, "I'm just mopping a dirty floor." Or you can say, "I'm keeping this residential center clean because without this work, this place would become disease-ridden for the patients who already struggle with so much."

You can say, "I'm cleaning up poop in a horse barn. This is the worst." Or you can be aware that if you don't, the horses' hooves and lungs will soon suffer.

So often our "menial" jobs are important works of mercy.

I'm naturally a little lazy and a lot selfish. Every job I've ever had, from working in a factory to working in fields to mopping floors, has forced me out of my usual pattern in order to be a blessing to people.

Never look down on your job. Serving people is not humiliating. It's ennobling.

Work is a very good thing. It's not a punishment from God. It's not the result of the fall of man. It was part of the perfection of Eden before the fall. God gave Adam a job to do from the very beginning. We need work to thrive, and almost all work is meaningful. Be thankful for it.

Never look down on your job. Serving people is not humiliating. It's ennobling.

Work is such a part of us that most of our hobbies are actually work. My main hobby (nerd alert) for years was the tabulation and organization of baseball statistics. I was essentially doing mathematical and actuarial work, coming up with algorithms and probabilities. Some people garden. Some people hunt.

Some people knit, and some do woodworking. I have a friend who loves to find scrap wood in dumpsters and make furniture from it.

We're so made for work, we can't stop. Even most video games are essentially about performing tasks and accomplishing virtual work.

If we *do* try to stop, we start to get restless. I'm serious about this. Watch some documentaries about retired athletes or people who win the lottery and retire early. They're not healthy. They thought they could just lie on the beach, but that's not what we're designed for. We can't do that and thrive.

If I have one regret about all the seemingly boring jobs I've had, it's that I didn't bring all my energy to them. They were repetitive and tiring, sure. Some days I'd come home listless and worn-out. But the solution to being tired isn't always taking a vacation. The solution is often bringing passion to the job.

One of my favorite comedians, Brian Regan, tells a story about working at a Walmart-type store. One day on the job, one of his coworkers excitedly whispered to him, "Hey, come here. Check this out!"

He led Brian to a hole in a wall behind the area where they assembled the bikes. No one could see them in there! They could get away with not working! They could spend the next six hours of their shift without doing anything!

They were also standing in a dark and cramped space. It was hard to breathe.

Brian asked, "Wait, why is this better than working? We're standing in a wall."

Valid point. Instead of working to avoid work, maybe just . . . work? There's a Scripture passage about this: "Whatever you do, work at it with all your heart, as working for the Lord, not for human masters, since you know that you will receive an inheritance from the Lord as a reward. It is the Lord Christ you are serving" (Col. 3:23–24).

Bring your all to what you're doing. It makes the time go faster. But even better, it's an act of worship. It's what you're made to do.

MAKE WOMEN AND CHILDREN FEEL SAFE, NOT THREATENED

How to Treat Women

The Bridger Master Class

We've already talked about why we need to be protectors of the gardens God puts us in, but what does that look like practically?

Sometimes it's the *really* young guys who show us how it's done.

There's an Instagram post that went viral in 2020 of a little boy and a tiny girl. He has his arm around her. They're cute, but that's not what you notice. What you immediately see is that the boy's face is severely lacerated. There's a massive cut from his swollen lip through his cheek all the way up to his swollen left eye. The entire left side of his face is wounded.

His name is Bridger, and he was playing with his four-year-old sister outside their home in Wyoming when a snarling German shepherd tried to attack her.

But Bridger stepped in.

Why'd he do it? After he got out of the hospital—ninety stitches later!—he told his dad, "I thought if someone should have to die, it should be me."[1]

Bridger gets it. And he's only six.

While the incident itself was profound, the reaction to it was too. The story was massive. It was on the national news and all the big network morning shows. It was shared tens of millions of times on social media. Hollywood even got involved: The cast of the Avengers movies sent Bridger gifts and connected with him in video calls. Chris "Captain America" Evans sent him his own shield.

When people see men (even six-year-old ones) doing what men are made to do, they sense that it's deeply right.

Bridger is a keeper of the garden. It's obvious his parents instilled this in him. I hope he keeps this mentality as he grows up, and I suspect he will. If he does, his sister will continue to respect him and feel safe around him. And you can bet his future wife and kids will too.

I'm trying to be this kind of man, a man who makes his wife feel secure and protected. I know my wife is every bit my equal. I know she's highly intelligent and strong and creative and funny. I know she can survive with or without me. But it's my goal to see her thrive and flourish. I believe in her so strongly, I'm excited about what she can still become.

Currently, Carolyn is a tutor and mentor to kids from difficult family situations. She's brilliant at it. I want to add value to what she does, help give her confidence, and be her biggest fan. I don't want to give her things to worry about in my own behavior.

I've learned that she loves it when I make her feel secure. She loves it when I'm consistently kind and controlled. She loves knowing that I'm not leaving. She loves that I don't flirt with other women. I want to make it obvious to her that of all the possible concerns in her world, she doesn't need to worry about what I'm up to or where I'm going. I'm not going anywhere.

I'm convinced that's my job as a husband. Does she wish I could fix cabinets and stuff? Sure, but it doesn't bother her much that I can't. She's mostly concerned that I care enough about the cabinets to get them fixed if they need it. It matters to her that if something matters to her, it matters to me too. (That's an awkward sentence, but I like it, so I'm keeping it.)

Another thing I've learned is that the things that seem small to me are often big things for Carolyn, and it's not because she's being illogical. If I leave my socks on the floor, it can seem like a dumb thing to argue about. They're just socks, right? But Carolyn told me something that stuck with me: It's not about the socks. It's about whether I care.

You'll find, if you get married, that "Do you still care? Do I still matter to you?" are always the key questions, even after many years.

This isn't just what insecure humans want to know. It's what all humans want to know, even secure ones. That's how marriage works, and I chose to get married. Marriage is intense.

But I'm learning—still learning!—about what it means to be a good husband and a good keeper of the garden, and about how to treat the women God gave me.

We want to learn from the best, of course. So I give you another master class . . .

How to Treat Women

The Jesus Master Class

Let's start with a quick look at how Jesus treated women. Since I'm an apprentice of Jesus, I want to learn how he does things and then do them myself. And here's what I'm learning:

1. Jesus respects women.

How he went about doing this was shocking in his day. In fact, it's *still* shocking in many traditional cultures.

There's a story that's familiar to many Bible readers, in which Jesus visits a pair of sisters, his friends Mary and Martha. Mary is sitting at his feet while he and his disciples talk. Martha is all about getting things ready. And she is mad. She complains to Jesus: "Tell her to help me!" But Jesus says that what Mary is doing is better. (See Luke 10:38–42.)

The takeaway from this story that I was always taught was this: Mary is willing to take time out to spend time with Jesus, but Martha is just too busy. Jesus teaches her a lesson about her busyness.

But that isn't the whole story, as it turns out.

I realized this in my own travels. In some cultures, I've been in homes where I don't see the women. They stay in the kitchen. Only the men are allowed to sit in the living room or dining room on the floor. When food is served, it's slid under a curtain into the room where we men are congregating. Or children are allowed to bring it in.

But catch what Jesus does here. He has arrived with his own group of men, and they're talking in another room, likely waiting for the meal to come.

Mary joins them. She sits with them—the men—at the feet of Jesus.

Jesus doesn't send her away. She belongs.

This may seem inconsequential to you, but I can tell you, in the environments I've been in, this would have been strange and, to many, offensive behavior. Mary is doing something radical for that time and place, but Jesus says she's doing the right thing, and he's got her back.

2. Jesus actively listens to women.

Another famous story in John 4 involves Jesus and a woman with an embarrassing reputation. He encounters her at the well where she gets water outside her village. John notes that the meeting happens around noon. It's possible that the woman's reputation is so bad and she is such an outcast that she has to go to the well during the middle of the day to avoid being with others. But Jesus talks to her. He listens to her. Intently.

She's taken by surprise. Not only is she a woman, and one with a bad reputation, but she is also a Samaritan. All these things added up mean she fully expects to be ignored.

Jesus' disciples are off getting some lunch, and when they come back, they're "surprised to find him talking with a woman" (John 4:27). At the time, Jesus is likely dealing with all the things that normally lead us to fail and make excuses. He is probably tired, hungry, thirsty, and lonely. But he still honors her. She finds that she has no reason to feel threatened. Not only does he not take advantage of her or diminish her, but he empowers her.

You can read the whole story, but let me spoil the ending. This woman starts to believe that Jesus may be the Messiah. She runs into her village to tell people about him. They invite Jesus to stay with them, and after he does, many of them become believers.

There have been hundreds of thousands, maybe millions, of missionaries who have gone into communities to tell people about Jesus of Nazareth.

But the first missionary in history . . . was a woman.

3. Jesus defends women.

There are various ways he does this, but I want to home in on one particular event when a woman was caught in the act of adultery, which carried a death sentence.

Jesus is teaching in the temple courts at the time, so the religious leaders decide to trap him. Their laws call for the shamed woman to be stoned, but what does he think should happen?

Jesus defends her.

He doesn't do it with a supernatural show of power or muscle, though he certainly could have. He uses his intelligence. He uses his words.

He essentially tells the men, the religiously correct stone holders, "Go right ahead and stone her . . . as long as you haven't sinned."

I imagine there's silence and confusion, followed by the sound of stones dropping. And maybe some muttering as the men scatter. They all leave. The woman is left with Jesus.

> Jesus . . . asked her, "Woman, where are they? Has no one con-demned you?"
>
> "No one, sir," she said.
>
> "Then neither do I condemn you," Jesus declared. "Go now and leave your life of sin." (John 8:10–11)

Once again, Jesus is giving us a brilliant picture of masculinity done right. Where Adam had failed (by letting a woman face an enemy without saying a word), Jesus rises to this woman's defense and sends her enemies scurrying away.

Think about this: Our culture specializes in *uncovering* shame—particularly that of women—explicitly for the disordered delight of others. Uncovering shame diminishes and exposes and dehumanizes.

But Jesus stands up to that culture and *covers* shame.

If you're going to be like him, you'll do the same.

Understand What "Love" Is and Isn't

People use the word "love" a lot. But honestly, what is it?

A friend might say to you, "I love this woman I just met," and he might mean a hundred different things. He might mean, "She attracts me," "She makes me laugh," "She makes me feel good," "She makes me feel important," or "She excites me."

All this "love" can be roughly distilled into one idea: *I love how I feel*. Or, even more briefly: *I love me*.

That's it. Most of the time, when we use the word "love" in our culture, we're talking about our love for ourselves. The other person is a means to an end. *I am a consumer, and if she provides what I'm looking for, I will continue to consume what she can offer. But if she ceases to provide the good self-feelings, well, I must not love her anymore.*

We use the word "love" this same way to describe experiences. Someone might say, "I love going to a Nickelback concert." (That's a throwback inside joke for us older people.) Why? Because they like the feelings they experience when the band hits the distortion in "Photograph."

Or we use it to describe authors: "I love J. R. R. Tolkien." (And boy, do I ever.) Why? Because of the entertainment he provides me, the "aha" insights I gain from him, the vicarious adventure, and the sense of togetherness I feel when I read his stories of fellowship or about his friendship with C. S. Lewis.

I even use the word "love" to describe food: "I love pizza." Do I want to see pizza reach its full potential? Will I sacrifice myself to protect it? Am I interested in its long-term good? No. By "love," I mean I want to rip it apart and digest it. By "love," I mean I want to wring every possible good feeling I can from its warm, tangy, cheesy, crusty goodness. I want the feelings it gives me. And if it's destroyed in the process, well, fine. In fact, I'll destroy it *because* I "love" it.

This is a common way men treat women, as things to be consumed and experienced. If she doesn't provide the feelings we're after, we move on.

This is a betrayal of our God-given role as keeper of the garden. When we treat women like consumable objects, we are doing the work of the enemy. We become destroyers and predators instead of protectors.

So what is love, really?

Our culture has equated "love" with unquestioning approval of someone else's decisions. But we all know that's not true. For example, saying "I love you, so I will cheer on your drug addiction!" makes no sense. If something is ultimately harmful for you, my approval isn't love at all. It's closer to hate.

So here you go, the best definition of real love I've ever heard: *Love is wanting what's truly best for others.*

If you do not desire that for someone, you do not love that someone. It's that simple. You may say you love them. You may think you love them. But you don't truly love them.

> **When we treat women like consumable objects, we are doing the work of the enemy. We become destroyers and predators instead of protectors.**

The point of real love is to want your loved one to thrive and flourish, even to the point of self-sacrifice. This is the kind of love that sees potential and promise even if the person you love may not see those things in themselves.

If you have this love toward a woman—the kind that's excited when she continually grows and shares her intelligence and gifts with the world—you have the makings of a potentially fantastic husband. You'll know you love a woman when you want to see her become everything she can be, even if it means your own inconvenience or hardship.

A woman is not a product to be consumed. If you're going to use the word "love," if you tell a woman that you love her, remember this: At the very heart of love, real love, is security.

If your "love" for a woman dies when she fails to give you good feelings, you didn't love her; you loved you.

But if you stick it out, even when the good feelings aren't present, well . . . now we're talking.

Protect Them . . .
from You

This chapter is about gentleness, and I can guess the response because I'd be thinking it: "Let me guess: I should be gentle. Yes. I got it. I can skip this."

But please don't skip this chapter. Read it because it's probably not exactly what you think. Also, I'm trying hard to write it up real good for you. All this work laboring over a hot computer and you just skip the chapter? No sir.

As I mentioned, I'm not the classic manly guy. As a flute-playing, non-hunting, can't-fix-anything kind of guy, I don't have a particularly negative reaction to being told that I need to be gentle.

After all, I've never abused anybody. I've never been a bully. I've never been a guy who hurts vulnerable people. I don't injure people. That's not how I roll.

The only problem is this: Every sentence I wrote in the previous paragraph is a lie.

I *have*, in fact, abused people. I *have* been a bully. I *have* been a guy who hurts vulnerable people.

Oh yes, I've done it and sometimes continue to do it. I do it with my words.

I'm a master of this, sadly. Most people are, I think. Like Dallas Willard has pointed out, we bless or curse people in every interaction with them, and even the slightest pause in a conversation can be a curse. (For example: "Do you love me?" Pause, slightly longer-than-normal breath. "Sure I do.")

We must become attuned to how we use our words if we are going to be keepers of the garden around us. Our friends, enemies, siblings, teachers, coworkers—even our bosses—are often at the mercy of our words and our blessings and curses.

A gentle gardener knows he can easily kill a beautiful, precarious, precious new growth poking out of the soil. But he doesn't do it.

(By the way, I know that one popular definition of a "gentleman" is "a man who can play the accordion but doesn't." As an accordion player, I reject this.)

To be a gentle man is to be the sort of guy who is more than capable of hurting the weak . . . but doesn't do it. Look at Jesus as the example of living this out. The prophet Isaiah describes the Messiah in this way:

> A bruised reed he will not break,
>   and a smoldering wick he will not snuff out.
> In faithfulness he will bring forth justice. (Isa. 42:3)

Jesus calls himself gentle. "I am gentle and humble in heart," he says (Matt. 11:29). Anyone who trusts him will find rest. He won't hurt us. We can be around him and we won't feel threatened. We can relax. This is how the vulnerable should always feel around us.

As a reminder, we're talking about the King of Kings. He is not lacking in power or the willingness to use it. In Revelation 1, he's described as having eyes "like blazing fire" and a voice "like the sound of rushing waters." He holds the stars, shines like the sun, and holds the keys to death itself. He's also got a sword "coming out of his mouth," which I can't quite picture, but it's awesome that he can do that. (See vv. 12–18.)

All that and he's gentle and humble in heart? This sounds like a guy to emulate, the ultimate keeper of the garden.

Weirdly, we all have "swords" in our mouths in the sense that we can cut people mercilessly with the words we choose to use. We can leave them on the floor, bleeding from spite or carelessness.

It's likely that there are people you could talk to right now and damage permanently if you so desire. Your power is scary. Be gentle. Don't betray your role.

Stay silent when needed, but never passive. Actively decide to wield your words carefully. Wield them to always defend and never wound the vulnerable people around you.

> **Stay silent when needed, but never passive. Actively decide to wield your words carefully. Wield them to always defend and never wound the vulnerable people around you.**

You should know that being gentle is very hard for me. Not only did I grow up the nerdy sort, but I was also physically small with a neurological disability that practically begged to be made fun of by elementary, middle, or high school guys. To make things worse, we moved often during my school days, so I repeatedly found myself exposed to entirely new batches of potential jerks.

My means of defense? My words. I was a quick thinker, and my verbal sword became razor sharp. It's how I survived. Want to make fun of the little kid with the shaking head? You can, but know that you will be quickly mocked, spectacularly and publicly, in front of your classmates. People will think you're stupid because Brant will diminish and demolish you with his put-downs.

Words are my thing. They might be yours too. Most of us don't have the problem of routinely hitting people at school. (If this *is* your problem, let me know, and my smash follow-up book will be called *Hey Guys, Stop Hitting People at School*.)

Be gentle with your words.

In his excellent book *The Masculine Mandate*, Richard D. Phillips shares a revelation from a friend. It has stuck with me, and I hope it sticks with you.

I used to think that if a man came into my house to attack my wife, I would certainly stand up to him. But then I came to realize that the man who enters my house and assaults my wife every day is me, through my anger, my harsh words, my complaints, and my indifference. As a Christian, I came to realize that the man I needed to kill in order to protect my wife is myself as a sinner.[1]

Yes, we must protect. And it starts with protecting the vulnerable people around us . . . from us.

Body, Mind, and Soul

I had a conversation with a caller on my radio show. He started with, "I live with my girlfriend. We know we're going to get married someday. So what's the difference, really? It's just a piece of paper."

"Okay, so, honest question," I said. "What's stopping you from getting married?"

"What do you mean?"

"Honestly, what's stopping you from marrying her right now?" I genuinely was curious. "You say you're committed to her. You're giving her your body, and you're taking hers. So why not take a vow in front of her family and friends and yours?"

"Finances, I guess."

"But you live together. What's more expensive about living together as a married couple?"

"I don't know," he said. "I mean, I just want to make sure I can provide for her and my son."

"So you've got a son with her?"

"Yeah. He's two."

"You say you want to provide for him. Why not provide him and his mom with the security of a man who is never going to leave?" I asked. "Why are you writing checks with your body that your soul won't cash?"

"I hadn't thought about it that way. I think you're right."

"Really?"

"Yeah, I think you're right. I think I just didn't want to take responsibility. I think I need to step up."

"I think you're my new hero," I said. "Very few guys will rethink like that. Much respect."

Our culture believes it's perfectly beneficial for a couple to live together without marriage. But guess what? A woman wants her man to commit to her.

Make no mistake about this. A man's commitment provides security and reassurance in a chaotic world. A woman doesn't want him to use her body while he keeps his options open. That should go without saying, I suppose—like much of this book—and yet it still needs to be said.

Man and woman are created in the image of the Creator. Genesis 1:27 says,

> God created mankind in his image,
> in the image of God he created them;
> male and female he created them.

That means sex is an act of re-creation. Something very mystical and deep is happening for both male and female. It's a coming together of two facets of God's image.

Jesus says this is why marriage exists, to bring together male and female as one:

> "Haven't you read," he replied, "that at the beginning the Creator 'made them male and female,' and said, 'For this reason a man will leave his father and mother and be united to his wife, and the two will become one flesh'? So they are no longer two, but one flesh. Therefore what God has joined together, let no one separate." (Matt. 19:4–6)

It's common in our culture for people to live together without getting married. But think about it: If you decide to have a sexual relationship with a woman without marrying her, you're acting out this mystical "one flesh" with your body but not with your soul. You're valuing keeping your options open more than you are valuing her. You're taking her without fully giving yourself.

If you decide to have a sexual relationship with a woman without marrying her, you're acting out this mystical "one flesh" with your body but not with your soul.

You're also acting in a way that will be your undoing. You will disintegrate—literally, dis-integrate. It's the opposite of integrity, a falling apart that happens when the body, soul, and mind are acting out of order with each other.

You may also be contributing to your girlfriend's dis-integration. Your body is proclaiming oneness with and protection for her, but the rest of you isn't. You're acting out a lie.

Sex in the context of commitment—body, soul, and mind—is creative and secure. Sex out of that context is the opposite. It's destructive to her and to you. You can "make it work" for a while outwardly, but ultimately, acting in dis-integrity corrodes all facets of life.

The guy I talked to on the phone called me back the next week. He and his girlfriend had gotten married. Apparently, she was just waiting for him to act. Again, I have a lot of respect for the guy taking responsibility for the woman he loved and the little boy who needed the security of a home with mom and dad forever. That's a very good thing.

Body, mind, and soul—all together now. That's integrity.

CHOOSE TODAY WHO YOU WILL BECOME TOMORROW

Attention Is Everything

Who we become is within our control. It's not a mystery. It's predictable. How?

Who we become is a direct result of what we pay attention to.

You should highlight that. Go ahead, I'll wait here. Don't make me come highlight it for you. (Headline: "Author Convicted of Breaking and Entering in Bizarre Highlighting Case.")

It's that important.

"The life we live out in our moments, hours, days, and years, wells up from a hidden depth," wrote Dallas Willard. "What is in our 'heart' matters more than anything else for who we become and what becomes of us."[1]

We're all emotional beings, and we can't always control our emotions. But what we *think about* has a tremendous effect on our emotions, and we do have a great deal of control over what we think about.

Yes, we live in a culture that pushes all sorts of foolishness and evil at us, constantly pinging our eyes, ears, and brains with banner ads and notifications and billboards and commercials and social media posts and messages. It's a bombardment. But taking responsibility for ourselves starts with us. We have to stand guard over our own minds.

Set your minds on things above, not on earthly things. . . . Put to death, therefore, whatever belongs to your earthly nature: sexual immorality, impurity, lust, evil desires and greed, which is idolatry. Because of these, the wrath of God is coming. You used to walk in these ways, in the life you once lived. But now you must also rid yourselves of all such things as these: anger, rage, malice, slander, and filthy language from your lips. (Col. 3:2, 5–8)

I used to see Scriptures like this and think, *Yes, yes, sure . . . but that's not entirely realistic.* But dealing with my impurity, lust, greed, anger, rage, and so on is not unrealistic at all. Those all stem from what I'm consistently putting my mind on. What we pay attention to is everything.

What we pay attention to is everything.

And when I say "pay attention," notice how the word "pay" fits. Our attention is a limited thing, and we have to manage it like finances. When I'm paying attention to something, I'm buying a ticket so my brain can attend.

Marketers know that what we pay attention to absolutely influences our emotions and behavior. In fact, they know that if we as consumers see a particular advertisement over and over, we are more likely to view the product as "high quality"—simply because we keep encountering the ad.[2] At some level we think, *This must be a great product, or they wouldn't keep showing it to me.* The very fact that our attention keeps being drawn to something suggests that it's an important and valuable something, even if it's not.

We all have desires, of course. But what we pay attention to has an enormous impact on how those desires get fueled.

As powerful as our desires are, they don't need to define us or control us. They really aren't all-powerful, after all. Our desires are not the last word about who we are. That's really good news.

Life is hard enough without us actively going out of our way to throw kerosene on our already burning desires. If I'm addicted to, say, FUNYUNS, maybe using my free time to peruse FUNYUNS commercials on YouTube is not an effective way to address this. If I know I've been drinking too much, maybe putting a poster of a delicious, sweating pint o' Guinness on my wall is a bad idea. If I realize I'm way too angry about current events, why poke the Anger Bear with the stick of "news" and opinions I know will make it worse?

(I totally just used the words "FUNYUNS" and "Anger Bear" in the last paragraph, and I just want to take a moment to bask in that. Thank you.)

Anyway, you get my point. If I want to shape who I'm becoming, I've got to put my mind on other things, better things, and I actually *can* do that.

I am responsible for what I do with my thoughts. I can take them captive, Scripture says, and break them like an experienced rider can break a wild horse. As Paul wrote to the Corinthians, "We take captive every thought to make it obedient to Christ" (2 Cor. 10:5).

Do evil, foolish, or just plain dumb thoughts pop into my head? Oh, heck yes, they do. But I can recognize what they are and move on. I can replace those thoughts with better ones. I can get busy doing something else. I don't have to beat myself up for stuff that pops into my head.

When I get negative, intrusive thoughts, there are decisions I can make to move on from them. I *have* to move on, or I will never be the man I need to be for others.

I can't mess this one up. Everyone around me is depending on it. It's the same with you. What you pay attention to will affect the people around you, for good or ill.

If the keeper's heart is lost, the garden is lost too.

Remember, Foolishness = Pain

If you want to become the you we need you to be, hang out with people you know who also want to be the people we need them to be. (You should know that when I started that sentence, it made sense in my head, I promise you.)

Here's what I mean: Don't be friends with fools. Pick some non-fools.

"Fool" has specific meanings in the wisdom literature of the Bible. You can read Proverbs yourself, and you should, but I'll give you a quick rundown on what fools do:

They love to vent their anger (29:11).

They don't want wisdom (1:7; 23:9).

They don't learn their lessons. They keep saying and doing the same destructive stuff over and over (26:11).

They hate real knowledge of God (1:22).

They don't want to understand . . . because they're too busy telling you their opinions (18:2).

They can't handle discipline (15:5).

They're quick-tempered (12:16).

They tend to get into a lot of arguments (18:6–7).

They mock people who take repentance seriously (14:9).

You: Hey Brant, you know you just described social media, right?

Me (looking at list again): Wow, you're right. Nice catch. And a great point too, because of what Proverbs 13:20 says:

> Walk with the wise and become wise,
>   for a companion of fools suffers harm.

We cannot exempt ourselves from this. A common cognitive bias leads us to think, *I'm not being influenced by this message, but other people are.* It's called the "third-person effect." It makes the vast majority of us think advertising works on other people but not us.

The truth is that, like me, you are influenced by the company you keep, and that includes intellectual company, for good or ill. If you read a lot of C. S. Lewis, you will begin to think like him. If you spend your time consuming angry political commentary, you'll likely be angrily thinking more about politics.

A companion isn't merely someone you're physically hanging out with. It's whoever or whatever has your attention.

Spend time in venues loaded with wisdom? Get wiser.

Spend lots of time on social media? Get more foolish.

And get hurt too. Here's another Proverb, and it's become one of my favorites since I discovered it twenty minutes ago when I was searching the word "fool" in the Bible. Why do I like it so much? Bears.[1]

> Better to meet a bear robbed of her cubs
>   than a fool bent on folly. (17:12)

So you can hang out with fools if you'd like. But for the record, you're better off being mauled by an enraged mama bear. You know it's serious business when the Proverbs writer brings up enraged mama bears.

Ask God for wisdom. It's one of the most important things you can request, and he promises he'll give it to you. Wisdom will spare you and others around you immense pain. That's the thing about foolishness: It always, always, always brings pain.

Wisdom is knowing what matters. Wisdom is understanding the true value of things.

What's worth more: the thrill of knocking back an entire box of chocolate donuts, or your fitness goals?

What's worth more: the fun of staying up until 3:00 a.m. to play a game, or being able to function for a big exam at school tomorrow?

Sometimes it's not so obvious, of course. But wisdom always helps. Always.

What's worth more: the rush you get from being "right" in the moment, or protecting the long-term relationship with this person you say you love?

What's worth more: learning your lesson now and suffering a bit of an ego blow, or refusing to be corrected so that you keep making the same mistakes, no matter how costly?

Wisdom is more precious than anything else you can ask for because life is almost nonstop decisions. Some psychologists estimate we make 35,000 decisions a day.[2] Imagine making those decisions while starting from a skewed view about what really matters in life.

Wisdom is more precious than anything else you can ask for because life is almost nonstop decisions.

I once saw a car race—I'm not making this up—that was a *blindfold* race. The drivers weren't allowed to see. It was on an oval racetrack near Orlando as part of a night of races aptly called "Crash-A-Rama." I can provide documentation on demand.

Anyway, each car had a passenger who was supposed to describe to the driver what to do. ("EDDIE, TURN LEFT NOW!!!") The race was set for ten laps.

Now, you might think there's no way this could work, that no one would be stupid enough to wear a blindfold and hit the gas when they heard the starting gun. But you'd be wrong, because they totally did, and lo, the lead cars plowed into the wall at the first curve! Everybody got hurt, and a helicopter had to be called in to take people to the hospital. I felt vaguely guilty for being there, and I'm pretty sure my IQ just now dropped six points from thinking about it.

The race lasted a quarter lap.

Living life without wisdom is like . . . that. If I don't have wisdom, I don't know where the heck I'm going. The crash is coming. It's just a matter of time.

Ask for wisdom. Why not? And if you really want it, make the wise your companions. You'll become like them. Their thinking will shape yours. They will help you order—or reorder—your values and desires. They will affect your attitude toward life itself. Do not underestimate this.

We need men with wisdom. In fact, we're desperate for them.

Walmart Shopping Cart Attack Guy Never Set Out to Be Walmart Shopping Cart Attack Guy

So, a related question: What kind of man do you want to be in your old age?

(A) A secure, peaceful, strong man who is good-humored, is attentive to others, listens intently, offers insight, and is a source of wisdom and hope.

(B) One of those cranky old guys who hits you with his shopping cart at Walmart.

There's no "right" answer, even though we're all hoping you don't choose Walmart Shopping Cart Attack Guy. But this really is a Choose Your Own Adventure kind of decision. It's not just a thought exercise.

We're always becoming something. I've had to realize that each decision I'm making now is shaping that future old guy. I want to wind up like Gandalf, a man of action who is wise and learned, with a twinkle in my eye and an awesome horse. I plan to also name my awesome horse Shadowfax.

Abraham Lincoln has been reported to have said, "Every man over forty is responsible for his face."[1] When I first heard that quote, I thought, *That's actually pretty raw of Abraham Lincoln to say. Not fair.*

But he was onto something. We create ourselves over time. We are becoming something, and that something is more and more pronounced the older we get.

People don't generally think, *You know what? I want to become a nasty, embittered, miserable old person.* But it happens nonetheless, based on a lifetime of decisions that started when they were much younger.

We're all becoming something, and we need to be careful about what that is. We can harbor selfishness and bitterness at nineteen and possibly get away with it while we're still youthful. But over time, it will shape us and misshape us.

Think about this like launching a rocket to the moon. The trajectory may be just one degree off at takeoff, and no onlookers will pick up on it. People applaud and finish their picnics. No big deal, right?

Except the rocket will now miss the moon by 4,100 miles.

Just a one-degree difference, and with time and distance, it's not even close.

God is very interested in who we are becoming. In fact, that's his central concern with us. We will either be more like him and an oasis of peace and strength for others in a chaotic world, or be a twisted grumble machine.

You are setting your trajectory even now. Do not discount the impact of the decisions you are making.

You are setting your trajectory even now. Do not discount the impact of the decisions you are making. Not only do we need you today; we're going to need you later to be the man God has in mind.

This doesn't mean you have to become Gandalf. (In fact, please don't, because that's kinda my thing. Pick another thing. It'll be embarrassing if we both show up at a party wearing the same hat-and-cloak combo.) But the world is starved for seasoned, other-centered men who can offer guidance and deep kindness.

How do I know this? *I'm* starved for it. I wish there were more men a generation older than me who weren't collapsed inwardly, unwilling (and frankly, apparently unable) to offer themselves for others.

I could write another book called *The Old Men We Need Right Now*, but it's likely too late. It's up to the rest of us to become those guys, and we need to start right now.

There are exceptions, of course. There are some older men providing examples of who we want to be, and the examples they give us are striking and beautiful.

I have a wise older friend who has eight children, all grown. Most of them are married with kids. It's a huge group, and they all love coming back home to get together. My friend loves seeing them, but as an introvert, it almost overwhelms him. Even so, it's remarkable to see the photos of everyone gathered around him. It reminds me how a man can be like an oak tree. Solid and enduring and able to shelter so much beautiful life.

Or maybe "foundation" is a better word picture. In construction, so much is dependent on the foundation. Even the most magnificent structure above it will crumble if it fails. But few notice it.

I'm a history nerd who's been to Notre Dame, the Roman Colosseum, and Windsor Castle, and I've never heard any tourists talking about the amazing foundations. I never even thought about their foundations until now, actually, and that's just the point. Men who are honorable serve as foundations for their families and communities, though they may never be fully appreciated.

Are you ready for that? I want to become a guy who can handle that. Maybe we're not there yet, but the exciting thing is who we can become: solid foundations for our family, our friends, our neighborhoods.

Let's do it.

"That's Awesome—
and I Don't Have to Have It"

The Ambition for Contentment

Today I was walking my dog, and I saw an awesome car sitting behind a neighbor's garage. It was a black Porsche Carrera. Unbelievably cool. I've long loved the design of that car. It's stunning.

For a second, I thought, *You know, I could get one of those.* Then I caught myself and reverted to another thought, one that's been extremely helpful in my life. I use it all the time. The thought is countercultural and at the very heart of wisdom in some ways.

Here it is: *Wow, that's awesome! And I don't have to have it.*

I highly recommend this little mental maneuver. And not just for nice cars either. Maybe it can be applied to somebody else's girlfriend. *Wow, she's attractive. And I'm not going to pursue her or fantasize about her. I don't need to possess everything that's beautiful.*

Or maybe it's someone else's tech gear or sweet job, or the exotic trips they get to go on. *Wow, that's amazing. And I don't need it.*

In America, we're taught that we're supposed to seek to possess everything we desire. It helps drive our economy. This is why some will read what I'm writing here and have a negative reaction. "You're saying it's bad to have a nice boat or something?"

No, I'm not saying that. I'm saying it's bad to be discontented. Or, better put, it's fantastic to be content, boat or no boat.

Contentment brings freedom. Discontentment makes you dependent. "If I can't have this thing/person/fame/whatever, I won't be satisfied" is a dumb way to live. If you *do* get that thing, chances are it won't satisfy you for long. If you don't get it—or if you lose it—you'll never be happy.

God included this wisdom in the Ten Commandments: "You shall not covet your neighbor's house. You shall not covet your neighbor's wife, or his male or female servant, his ox or donkey, or anything that belongs to your neighbor" (Exod. 20:17).

God isn't stupid. He didn't include this commandment because he was struggling to come up with a final one to make an even ten. ("I can't just leave it at nine, you guys.") He's telling us this—he's telling *you* this—to let you know some amazingly good news: If you trust God, if you live your life with him as King, you lack nothing. You can go anywhere. You can endure way more than you think. This is key to being ambitious about the right things. There's so much we don't need.

If you trust God, if you live your life with him as King, you lack nothing. You can go anywhere. You can endure way more than you think.

Once, I was part of a team of people trying to help victims of the tsunami in Indonesia. The problem was, after I'd traveled a brutal, sleepless thirty-eight hours to get to Medan, Indonesia, I found out there wasn't a ticket for me to fly the rest of the way to Banda Aceh. So my team leader put me in the cab of a dump truck headed that way.

It was a thirteen-hour drive overnight.

On a bench seat.

With four other dudes.

Who were smoking.

I sat on the end, squished against the door. I rolled the window down and hung my head out to avoid the cigarette smoke and breathe in the fresh, clean exhaust from the highway.

That might sound like hell on earth. Thirteen additional sleepless hours after a series of flights. No real food to eat. No escape from the smoke and the language barrier.

But here's the wild thing: I survived. I put up with it. I handled it. I surprised myself. I didn't even whine that much.

It's freeing to find out you really don't need very much, that you can put up with a lot. Perhaps you've had experiences like that too. Probably not *exactly* like that, though. If you say you had the same five-guys-in-an-Indonesian-dump-truck experience, I will question you.

David writes this in his famous Psalm 23: "The Lord is my shepherd, I lack nothing" (v. 1). *Nothing.* I have everything I need in order to do what I have to do today.

"He makes me lie down in green pastures," David continues (v. 2). As a shepherd himself, David knew that sheep only lie down (quit grazing) in tasty green pastures on one condition: They're full. Contentment is a real thing.

I'm not against Porsche Carreras, by the way. Maybe I'll have one someday. (It would be highly unlikely but ironically funny. If I do get one, I'll let you know. My next book will be titled *No Way: I Totally Got the Porsche, You Guys.*)

Wonderful things are, you know, wonderful. But I don't have to have them. That other radio guy gets a lot of attention? Let him have it. My friend has a pool? Sweet. I'll bring my dog and splash around in it. My neighbor has a beautiful wife? Good for him and her. That guy has better puppet skills than me? Okay, now we have a problem. But the point is, I'm working on it.

I have what I need. The Lord is my shepherd, after all. I lack nothing.

Seriously, try it. One of the most freeing, countercultural things you can say is "Wow, that's awesome—and I don't have to have it."

Become a Man without Fear (Seriously)

Fear can stop you from becoming the man you want to be. But you know what? You actually have nothing to fear.

Nothing.

This sounds preposterous to most people. It seems obviously wrong. In fact, most people are driven by fear. They're shaped by it.

I'm sure it also sounded preposterous when Jesus told his followers they didn't need to worry or be anxious about *anything* (see Matt. 6:25). How could he possibly say that?

Fear, after all, is one of the most basic human feelings.

"Ah, but it isn't for me," you may say.

"Yes, it is. Think about it," I'll respond. "The first thing you ever did was cry."

Stunned by the truth of my retort, you acknowledge that I totally just won the conversation.

It's true—everyone comes into the world crying and screaming. It's like we're all born with a bucket list, and it's not a long one:

BUCKET LIST
1. Freak out.

Was Jesus out of his mind when he said not to be anxious? Or was he joking? His audience at the time had to wonder. They were occupied by the Romans. They faced injustice, racism, disease, and food insecurity.

Maybe you've heard this story recorded in Mark 4:35–41: Jesus is out on a boat with his disciples. A storm kicks up, and it is apparently bad enough that even the experienced fishermen among them are freaking out, thinking they're going to die. Jesus is in the back of the boat asleep. His friends are panicked, so they wake him up. "Don't you care if we drown?" they ask, no doubt annoyed that he can somehow sleep during all of this.

Jesus speaks. The water is immediately calm. Then he tells his friends he's disappointed in them. Why were they so afraid? It's like they'd learned nothing. They actually had nothing to fear, but they still didn't get it.

They failed the test. And it was a test, by the way. After all, the boat trip across the lake was Jesus' idea. He knew the storm was coming; he knew he'd be asleep.

They didn't need to be afraid of the storm. And not just because Jesus was in the boat. Even if the boat had sunk, they would be okay. Even if they had drowned, God was in control of the situation. No matter what.

Jesus really *was* saying they had nothing to fear. The entire Bible is very consistent about this. "If God is for us, who can be against us?" Paul says in Romans 8:31. In Philippians 1:21, he says that living is great, but dying is a win too: "To live is Christ and to die is gain."

If we fear God, we need fear nothing else.

Seriously, what can others do to us? If I may quote the words of '90s rock band P.O.D., "Is that all you got? I'll take your best shot."

Here's another throwback reference: the 2005 NCAA Tournament. I'm a University of Illinois alum, and I remember watching the game live with my kids when they were little. It was a battle for a spot in the Final Four. I was nervous.

Illinois struggled. With four minutes left, they were behind by fifteen. It was obviously over. I was bitterly disappointed and told my son we might as well shut it off, what's the point, and so on. I was acting like a baby.

My little boy didn't want to shut it off. And Illinois staged an epic comeback and won!

Death is the ultimate weapon of our spiritual enemy, but two thousand years ago, it was disarmed.

I watch a replay of the game on You-Tube every few years. It's still entertaining and there's still some tension, but it's a totally different experience. I don't get bitter and negative watching it. I don't roll my eyes like I did the first time and say, "This game is over. Forget it. Forget everything."

Why? Because I know how it ends.

And Jesus' words assure us that *he knows how it ends*.

Death is the ultimate weapon of our spiritual enemy, but two thousand years ago, it was disarmed.

God is ultimately going to take care of us. As Jesus said,

> Can all your worries add a single moment to your life? And if worry can't accomplish a little thing like that, what's the use of worrying over bigger things?
>
> Look at the lilies and how they grow. They don't work or make their clothing, yet Solomon in all his glory was not dressed as beautifully as they are. And if God cares so wonderfully for flowers that are here today and thrown into the fire tomorrow, he will certainly care for you. Why do you have so little faith?
>
> And don't be concerned about what to eat and what to drink. Don't worry about such things. These things dominate the thoughts of unbelievers all over the world, but your Father already knows your needs. Seek the Kingdom of God above all else, and he will give you everything you need.
>
> So don't be afraid, little flock. For it gives your Father great happiness to give you the Kingdom. (Luke 12:25–32 NLT)

Imagine actually living this way. Who does that? I mean, besides Tony Stark. I remember watching an *Iron Man* movie (I forget which one) and especially enjoying Stark's fun-loving quips when it looked like he was going to die. It's like he knew he'd be fine. It's total fiction, of course, but I honestly believe we could be like that too.

People are drawn to this sort of attitude. In a world of insecurity and threats, a secure man who helps others feel secure is very compelling. A keeper of the garden is a man who knows how it all ends, that nothing can separate us from the love of God.

While everyone else gets anxious, it's incredibly encouraging to see someone who takes Jesus seriously and really believes, "The world is a perfectly safe place for me to be. I know how it ends."

No matter what.

What's that? You say you can take my life?

No, you can't.

I already gave it away.

TAKE RESPONSIBILITY FOR YOUR OWN SPIRITUAL LIFE

What God Is Looking For

Loyalty

This chapter is incredibly important. It could be its own book. Maybe you'll write it someday. I'd buy it.

Growing up in American church culture, I wrestled with this question: *What is it that God actually wants from me?*

It was confusing because the answer seemed like a long, strange list. I was pretty sure God wanted me to evangelize, to share the good news. So that was it. That was what he wanted.

But I was also pretty sure he really wanted me to read the Bible. So those two things—evangelism and Bible reading—were what I needed to concentrate on.

Wait. Prayer. That's important. So really, three things.

Also, giving to the poor and that sort of thing. Maybe I could combine that with being an activist for the right causes. So four things, really.

But also serving at a church as a volunteer in some capacity. And giving money to the church. So there's a couple more. Plus joining a small group because community is important. And singing worship songs with people and listening to sermons are both big. So those two other things are vital too—don't forget those.

Plus getting baptized. And receiving communion. And attending Sunday school. And extra services for Easter.

I think we're at around thirteen things so far. So just concentrate on the 13 Big Things, and—

Wait, there's fasting. I think we're supposed to go without food. God wants that. So just concentrate on the 14 Big Things. Also, confessing sin.

So, yeah. The 15 Big Things.

Plus help at a soup kitchen.

To my great relief, I have realized over time that God really wants one thing from us, and this is it:

Loyalty.

A believing, trusting loyalty. And it's loyalty to him specifically. Loyalty through everything, no matter what. I am loyal to him because he is loyal to me.

I can get caught up in sin, in my own failures to love God and people the way he wants me to. But I will not slink away in shame. I will keep talking with him about what we are doing together in life.

Loyalty means I keep talking to God, I keep pursuing him, whether I'm in the mood or not. Yes, I can get caught up in sin, in my own failures to love God and people the way he wants me to. But I will not slink away in shame. I will keep talking with him about what we are doing together in life.

Like a lot of people, I have plenty of meetings on my calendar. But this meeting with God is one I do not want to miss. He is powerful, and he is on my side. Nothing is more important than him.

Don't miss the opportunity to talk with God. He (1) knows you better than you know yourself, (2) still loves you, and (3) will do things for you.

I'm thankful for Scripture like the Psalms precisely because I can see what a genuine, honest relationship with God looks like. Many of the Psalms are attributed to David, who failed God spectacularly in spite of everything God had done for him. But his passionate interactions with God and his steadfast loyalty continued.

Or look at Job. He said many dumb things, and God verbally blasted him for it, putting him in his place . . . right before he rewarded Job many times over. Why? Simple: Job remained faithful. He just kept interacting. He failed in many ways, sure, but he never stopped seeking God. He was loyal.

So you're a sinner? Yep, so am I. But we can't let our guilt push us away from God instead of toward him. We have to keep meeting with him in spite of ourselves.

Real, raw prayer—the kind where you're thinking about what you're saying—forces honesty. If your mind is engaged and you're not just defaulting to crutch phrases, you won't be trying to fool God. You'll know you can't. That's one reason passionate, engaged prayer is so healthy. It doesn't have to be for a half hour or even ten minutes. Sometimes a thirty-second prayer is spectacular when you really mean it. Just keep at it. Don't let go of God.

Loyalty doesn't get talked about much in church circles, but it should. The word that captures this steadfast loyalty best in Hebrew is *hesed*, and it's not used just once or twice but 246 times in the Old Testament. Most of the time, it's used to describe God's loyalty to his people. But it's also used to directly tell us what God wants from us, like in Micah 6:8. We're to act justly, love *hesed*, and walk humbly with God.

Yes, he loves everyone. But not everyone is loyal to him. Not everyone has said, "I'm in, I'm your disciple, and you are my authority, come what may." Not everyone wants to be loyal to him. Sadly, they're loyal to things that won't last and ultimately don't give life.

Of course, no chapter on loyalty is complete without a *Lord of the Rings* reference. Merry had to assure Frodo that yes, his friends were afraid too, but they weren't leaving him. No matter what happened. Ever.

> You can trust us to stick to you through thick and thin—to the bitter end. And you can trust us to keep any secret of yours—closer than you keep it yourself. But you cannot trust us to let you face trouble alone, and go off without a word. We are your friends, Frodo. Anyway: there it is. We know most of what Gandalf has told you. We know a good deal about the Ring. We are horribly afraid—but we are coming with you; or following you like hounds.[1]

God isn't looking for a scrubbed-up life. If that was his main goal for you, he could force it. He wants way more than that. He's looking for the real you to be loyal to the real him.

That's when the adventure begins.

Don't Confuse Your Emotions—
or Lack of Emotions—
with Spirituality

God is looking for loyalty. We know this because I just wrote an incredible, award-winning chapter about it. Living a life of loyalty is something we can do; it's not out of reach.

Here's even more good news: Being "spiritual" does not mean being emotional. If you don't get emotional about God or spiritual topics or worship music, it does not mean something is wrong with you.

Jesus talks very little about emotions. He talks a lot about something else: obedience. Obedience is what he expects from those who follow him.

He wants us to follow his way of living because it's the best way to live. Loving our enemies, praying for those who hurt us, trusting God rather than living in fear—this is the way to freedom.

Our culture tends to be very feelings-driven. We allow our feelings to determine reality. Jesus, however, is not feelings-driven.

If you do get emotional while worshiping God with others or by yourself, that's fine. But don't confuse emotions with loyalty and obedience to the Master.

(I wrote extensively about this in another book, *Blessed Are the Misfits: Great News for Believers Who Are Introverts, Spiritual Strugglers, or Just Feel Like They're Missing Something*, and I recommend you buy a copy of that book. Maybe seven of them, actually. No, thousands of copies. Build a fort with them. Thank you.)

Just because you don't "feel" God around doesn't mean he has left you. Our feelings come and go based on many things, like whether we're eating well, we're dehydrated, or we need a nap.

Just because you don't "feel" God around doesn't mean he has left you.

It's apparent from Scripture that God is very pleased when we obey, whether we're feeling it or not. And let's face it, so much of obedience is about acting in a manner directly *opposed* to our feelings. Who *feels* like praying for the people who are persecuting them? Who *feels* like blessing people who curse them? Who *feels* like turning the other cheek and letting some selfish, attacking fool dictate their next move?

Answer: exactly nobody. Nobody feels that way. Just like nobody feels like picking up their cross daily and living a life of radical forgiveness for the very people who don't deserve it.

But we should do it anyway. This is the stuff of mature manhood. It's also the stuff of relating to God in the way he wants us to.

Maybe you already know this: If we do something because we're expecting something in return, it's not out of love for anyone but ourselves. But if we do something in spite of ourselves . . . now we're talking love.

"If you love me," Jesus said, "keep my commands" (John 14:15). If I love God, I will do the things he wants me to do, even without the promise of an emotional payoff. The emotions, frankly, have nothing to do with my actions.

So if you're not particularly emotional about your faith, don't worry about it. That simply isn't the point. It does not diminish your faith. You have much to offer.

The spiritual life of your parents or siblings or friends may not look like yours. They might be more emotive or less. They may wish your spiritual life looked more like theirs, but don't get hung up on this. You are responsible for your own pursuit of God, your own willingness to obey.

The issue, as always, is making it your intention to continue walking with and obeying God, whether you feel like it or not. As James writes, "Do not merely listen to the word, and so deceive yourselves. Do what it says" (James 1:22).

I met a guy named Kevin who was attending the same church we were. He was a man's man. He worked at a factory. He hunted. He drove a motorcycle. Unlike me, he could fix things. He wasn't emotive, but his wife was. She was musical, artistic, and expressive. And she was frustrated by his apparent lack of "connection" to God.

I got to know Kevin because I needed him. I was helping the high school kids in the church plan a trip to Mexico to build a house. Lots of them wanted to go, but there was one problem: me. And my lack of ability to plan stuff or build stuff or even work the tool . . . things.

I asked Kevin to go, explaining my situation. I think he was kind of suspicious of a guy from church with no guy skills, whom he barely knew, begging him to do something so out of the usual for him. But I needed his skills big-time.

Kevin said yes, and he was amazing. Irreplaceable. There's no way we would have finished the house without him. He was a workhorse, using his knowledge, muscle, and determination to do what I—or a team of a hundred other flute-playing writers—couldn't.

He was an encouragement to the students with us. He set the tone at the worksite and helped people learn new skills. He was a superstar. The family receiving the house was overjoyed, and Kevin got to see the couple and their little girls move in. They wouldn't have had this shelter without his work.

He told me it was the best couple weeks of his life, and he finally saw that he had a place, a role, in the kingdom. Apparently, "worship" to him had been defined as attending a stage presentation or a loud worship-themed weekly concert. He didn't resonate with that. But this? This he understood. This was his way to worship.

So, yeah, Kevin is not emotive. He doesn't cry during the worship music. But he said yes and did his thing, and now a family he didn't know has a home.

We may have made "religion" a primarily emotional experience. But notice how James describes the religion that God wants: "Religion that God our Father accepts as pure and faultless is this: to look after orphans and widows in their distress and to keep oneself from being polluted by the world" (1:27).

Spirituality isn't measured in goose bumps.

You Know Enough to Act

The best way to learn is by doing. We all know that.

It's also true that the best way to avoid doing is learning. Here's what I mean: We often use lack of knowledge as an excuse to put off doing what we need to do. Some of us (this is definitely me) enjoy studying the stuff more than actually doing the stuff. Instead of writing this book, for instance, I'm constantly tempted to read more books about how to write books.

Learning is good, and any follower of Jesus will want to learn more about him, just as any hockey player will want to learn more about the game. But learning the game is not playing the game.

Paul writes to the believers in Rome, "I myself am convinced, my brothers and sisters, that you yourselves are full of goodness, filled with knowledge and competent to instruct one another" (Rom. 15:14). Seriously? "Filled with knowledge"? They were a new group of believers. They had exactly zero Christian colleges. No seminaries. No awesome, inspiring books like this one.

They didn't even have Bibles.

But Paul is telling them, "You know enough to do this."

You can study the wonders of God for the rest of your life and never run out of new and exciting discoveries. That's a wonderful part of life with God. Even Jesus was clearly committed to memorizing Scripture. He quoted it constantly. These are very good things.

But the real game starts here and now.

Playing the game is putting into practice what Jesus told us to do: Loving our enemies. Praying for people who persecute us. Forgiving people as we've been forgiven. Blessing those who curse us. Praying for God's kingdom on earth as it is in heaven. Putting off the tendency to store up things for ourselves and instead being wildly generous.

In Luke 10, an expert in the law asks Jesus what he needs to do to inherit eternal life. Jesus responds with a question: "What is written in the Law?" (v. 26).

The expert quotes Scripture: "'Love the Lord your God with all your heart and with all your soul and with all your strength and with all your mind'; and, 'Love your neighbor as yourself'" (v. 27).

Jesus tells him he's right on. But watch the move the expert makes immediately after: "He wanted to justify himself, so he asked Jesus, 'And who is my neighbor?'" (v. 29).

Suddenly the big expert has no idea what "neighbor" means. He'd rather keep this whole thing academic.

Jesus: Love your enemies.

Religious experts: Let's maybe study this first.

Jesus: If you don't forgive, you won't be forgiven.

Religious experts: Well, he doesn't mean it quite like that. There's a lot of nuance there.

Jesus: No, I meant that.

Religious experts: Let's study it.

Jesus: No, I just want you to do it.

Religious experts: What does "do" mean, really? In Aramaic?

Jesus: What in the world.

It reminds me of when I had an epiphany on a basketball court in middle school. During PE class, we'd get a chance to shoot around, and of course I would take (and miss) inventive trick shots. Shots from behind the backboard, half-court hook shots, and so forth, until it suddenly dawned on me, *I can't shoot free throws. I'm not even solid on lay-ups. Why am I doing trick shots when I can't make normal shots?*

Wait. Maybe it's because *I can't make normal shots.*

I think a lot of our intellectual lives can operate that way. Maybe we prefer debating ideas to actually acting on what we know. Or we enjoy making the stuff more complex than it needs to be so we can keep avoiding the fundamentals.

I love how quickly non-expert types in the Gospels and in Acts go from being relatively uneducated to full-throttle followers of Jesus. They just start following him. They start as his apprentices. Because that's the best way to learn.

Make no mistake, following Jesus means *doing the stuff*. Even if you're not steeped in religious training or you're absolutely brand-new to this following Jesus thing, you can start right now. You don't need to wait until you've reached some level of mastery over all the information.

Don't let others convince you that you're not enough, you don't know enough, or you don't have the expertise. You can do this today.

Don't underrate yourself. The best way to learn is by doing, and we need you to take the field.

The Dangerous Myth of "As Long As I'm Not Hurting Someone Else . . ."

I want to tell you about my friend Greg. He's one of my favorite people. He has a strong personality, and he'd tell you that he can be hard to take sometimes, but I don't think so. He says he has average intelligence, but he's really an intelligent guy.

I always enjoy hanging out with him. We laugh a lot. He's brutally and refreshingly honest. He's also a guy's guy who hunts and fishes and has a big truck. I just bought a used Honda Fit. But somehow we're friends.

Because he's about my age, he also grew up in an era of video games and easily accessible pornography. At some point in his college years, he could have said, "You know what? I'm going to hole up in my room and collapse inwardly. I'm going to just play games and amuse myself. As long as I'm not hurting someone else, what does it matter?"

But he didn't do that. Instead, he rose to the occasion and finished college. He then got into medical school (he says he still doesn't know how he made it) and worked very hard. He's now a pediatric cardiac anesthesiologist.

Greg is great at putting scared little kids to sleep and putting their parents at ease too. He has five kids of his own and a wife who respects him. Because of his desire to emulate Jesus, he's spent months traveling through developing nations (often taking his family), serving in hospitals for the poorest people in the world. He's provided first-class care to some of the most desperate little patients in the world and trained more doctors to do the same.

His field is tricky, and there are horrific consequences when the work is done poorly. There's no doubt his dedication and his willingness to be a keeper of the garden have saved the lives of the vulnerable.

So, the obvious question: If he had, in fact, collapsed inwardly and handed himself over to video games and porn, would it have "hurt" anyone?

Of course it would have, but he wouldn't have known it. We would have missed out on the man he was supposed to be.

It's not an exaggeration to say that because of the choices Greg made when he was younger, many moms and dads haven't had to attend funerals for their own children. When we men take our roles seriously, when we're at our best, those are the kinds of things that happen. Healing. Peace. Life.

And when we don't, distortion, anxiety, violence, and meaninglessness fill the gap.

No one operates in a vacuum. You are not an island. Just as we saw with "Jake" earlier in the book, the idea of "it's okay as long as I'm not hurting anyone" doesn't work as a way to see the world. It's too simplistic.

Even the sins in our head aren't private. Mine affect my attitude. They keep me from being concerned about other people. They make me a jerk in seemingly unrelated ways. ("Why's Brant being a jerk?" "Probably something seemingly unrelated.") And when that happens, I'm not the person I'm supposed to be. I'm less creative. I'm less joyful. I have less social energy. My patience is gone. I care less about my neighbors.

Jesus is, as always, brutally honest about our "private" thoughts. In Matthew 5, he makes it clear (using examples like murder and adultery) that we are responsible for our thoughts even if we don't commit the act. And then he says this in Matthew 15: "For from the heart come evil thoughts, murder, adultery, all sexual immorality, theft, lying, and slander. These are what defile you" (vv. 19–20 NLT).

What we think about and what we do, even in "private," ripples outward. There's no stopping it. In many cases, what starts as a private thought life or habit winds up destroying relationships and families, and the ripples radiate through generations.

I may think I can entertain sinful ideas and habits, but I find that I become a different person very quickly. I become less of who I could be, and the world around me suffers for it.

Or I can grow up and show up, start taking my thoughts captive, and continually point my heart and mind back to God. This will have a ripple effect too!

Yes, we're all sinners, but no one else will ever occupy the exact role you have. No one else will be placed exactly where you are and with your particular gifts, both now and in the future.

We need you to be the man you are made to be. Make no mistake, there is no "as long as I'm not hurting someone else . . ."

If you're not who you're made to be, it hurts you.

And it hurts us.

Boldly Ask God—
Sarcastically, If Necessary

Get ready for a true but weird story.

I'm simultaneously a little ashamed of it and elated by it.

Here's what happened. I was out running on a sunny day. I was doing something I rarely did then (though I do it all the time now): I prayed out loud. And I prayed sarcastically, which was also odd.

Now, you should know that at the time, we had two little kids and could only afford one car, so I had a hard time getting to work each day. So as I was running, I asked God again, out loud, "Could you please give us a car?"

I looked to my left and saw a man driving a Jeep Wrangler with the top removed. He looked super cool riding around with his little boy, about my son's age, in the Florida sun.

"And while you're at it, can you make it a convertible?" I actually said those words. To God. Again, it was sarcastic. I was making fun of myself for asking.

Whenever I tell people this story, I let them know that I would never tell someone to pray like this, as if God were some kind of vending machine. The free convertible request was my ironic sense of humor. I don't normally pray that kind of prayer and would never advise someone to start praying like that.

But . . . *someone gave me a convertible before the end of the day.*

Out of nowhere!

I'm not kidding. That actually happened.

Carolyn and I were newly part of a small Bible study for parents, just four youngish couples, and we met in a room in a church building. We barely knew the others. That very evening, Owen, one of the guys in the group, told me he had a weird thing happen. His in-laws had given a minivan to his family. They were glad to have it.

Then Owen said he felt like God wanted him to give me his car. We had never talked about cars before, but Owen was standing there saying his family didn't need three vehicles. Did we need a vehicle, by chance? And if we did, would I be okay driving a convertible?

Why, yes, I would be okay driving a convertible.

I was in disbelief at what was happening.

Owen drove me to his house while Carolyn headed home to relieve our babysitter. Owen got his stuff out of the trunk and glove compartment. I'm not sure I could have said anything. I think my mouth was hanging open.

The car was an Infiniti with 50,000 miles. "It runs great," he said, and he signed over his title. Within minutes I was driving with the top down through the warm night air. I couldn't believe it.

(I *still* can't believe it. I mean, what are the odds, without God's involvement in this?)

I arrived home and went upstairs, where the kids were in their bunk beds. They hadn't quite gone to sleep.

"Hey Justice, hey Julia . . . I want to tell you a story." Stories always got their immediate attention, especially when they weren't expecting one. "You know how we need a car, right?"

I told them I'd prayed for help. I'd actually asked God for a convertible. Out loud I'd asked him this. Today.

"And now I want you to come downstairs!"

They followed after me in their pajamas. Carolyn and I put them in the convertible, and we went for a ride under the stars. It's a night they haven't forgotten, and I certainly never will either.

Two takeaways from Brant's free convertible story:

1. This whole thing was against my theology.
2. My theology is often stupid.

Why is it stupid? Because God isn't a math equation. He refuses to be pinned down so easily. He will not be controlled, figured out, or reduced to the if-then predictability of binary code.

Does God answer sarcastic prayers? Of course not.

Except when he does.

Does God give out free convertibles? Of course not.

Except when he does.

Here's a takeaway you shouldn't take away, but I'll bet your mind went there: "Okay, so I'll sarcastically ask God for an awesome vehicle because apparently it works."

But "it" doesn't work. God does what he wants. Our attempts to make "it" work essentially reduce prayer to a magic spell. ("If I say such-and-such just so, this will happen!")

> **God isn't a math equation. He refuses to be pinned down so easily. He will not be controlled, figured out, or reduced to the if-then predictability of binary code.**

Actual relationships don't work that way. If, as a dad, I did something wonderful to surprise my daughter by meeting a need in a delightful way, I would be alarmed if she tried to repeat her actions in order to make "it" happen again. Wouldn't that be manipulation?

There is no "it." There is only a "he," and he wants us to relate to him with honesty and passion. Like this relationship really matters. Like he is listening and actually loves us.

I mentioned that I'm a bit ashamed of this story, and it's true. I'm ashamed because I feel silly. I did nothing to earn a car. This story is a seemingly childish one that doesn't make me seem very respectable.

But who cares, right? It happened, and mostly I think it's wonderful and funny.

Sometimes when I read about God's interactions with people in Scripture, I see unpredictability. One minute he's speaking through a burning bush. The next he's speaking through an old man. Then a king. Then a donkey.

I have learned to talk to God honestly. Brutally honestly. Out loud. I encourage you to do this too. It's central to taking responsibility for your own spiritual life. Ask, not just because he gives us stuff but because of these two things:

1. God loves you. And because of that, he'll do things.
2. If you don't ask, who will?

CONCLUSION

A Final Word about Adam . . . and Us

Here's another thing I'm asking for, and it's not a car.

I'm asking God to guide your path for the rest of your days. You may think, *How's that possible if you don't even know me?* If I were reading this, I might think that too. But I know that God hears us when we honestly ask for things and that our prayers carry a lot of weight.

I also know that God knows who you are. And he's on your side.

Here's another thing I know: As a human being, you struggle with a lot of things. You get bogged down in habits and desires that you know are ultimately destructive. For a lot of guys, it's pornography or alcohol, but it could be any number of things.

We can get so discouraged. We think God is angry with us or is walking away from us. So we wind up walking away from him in shame.

Please don't do that. Please know God is not disgusted by you. Please don't let shame stop you from growing in other areas of life. When you fall, get back up. When my kids were little and learning to walk, like any loving father I wasn't disgusted when they fell down. I was delighted to see them get back up.

You're a sinner? So am I. So let's keep meeting with God. Let's keep interacting with him.

Be honest. Ask God to make a way for you. I'm convinced he will. Ask him for wisdom and keep asking, no matter what.

Keep pursuing him, and don't let shame ever stop you. Be relentless.

You're a sinner? So am I. So let's keep meeting with God. Let's keep interacting with him.

Lately I've been memorizing Scripture, which is something I've not been good at before. But I love how punk rock it is. (Translation in my generation: something unfashionable, decidedly not mainstream, and totally bold and authentic.) When I memorize Scripture, no one can take it from me. It's in my head. It goes with me wherever I go. I can walk around, as I do, and recall it over and over.

I memorized Psalm 23 (it's just six verses), and it reminds me that I have everything I need for today, I have nothing to fear, God is guiding me through life, and he will never let me down—ever. His goodness and love will follow me all the days of my life.

No one can take that from me.

———

I hope this book has been helpful to you. I tried to jam as much wisdom and encouragement into it as I could. And I'd like to finish it where we started—with Adam—because his story reveals how good God is.

Yes, we know Adam blew it. He was given a job, and he failed. I can relate to the failure part. I presume you can too.

But you know what? There's more to the story than that.

A friend pointed something out to me the other day: Adam isn't just in the beginning of the Old Testament. He shows up in the beginning of the New Testament too.

He's in Luke 3, in the genealogy of Jesus (which I've always kind of skipped over, honestly). It says this:

> Now Jesus himself was about thirty years old when he began his ministry. He was the son, so it was thought, of Joseph,

the son of Heli, the son of Matthat,
the son of Levi, the son of Melki. (vv. 23–24)

On and on it goes, for seventy-seven generations! After all that, here's how it ends:

the son of Jared, the son of Mahalalel,
the son of Kenan, the son of Enosh,
the son of Seth, the son of *Adam*,
the son of God. (vv. 37–38, italics mine)

There's Adam again. *God's son.* Still.

Sometimes the Christian story can be confusing. I can find myself wondering all over again, *Why would Jesus do what he did for us? Why the cross? Why would he do that?*

And then I see Adam on this list. "The son of God."

Jesus didn't endure the cross for just any reason. No one does that. No, we only make that kind of sacrifice for family.

We are called to do Adam's job. We're keepers of the garden, protectors and defenders and coworkers in the kingdom of God. All the things I've asked you to consider in this book are vital for us and those around us.

But if you are also like Adam in that you've failed (and you have, and so have I), please take note of this: If there's an epitaph for Adam, and for you and me, it remains "a son of God."

God still claims us. He still wants us. He's still our Father, and he can help us change.

That's a strong, secure place to be.

Knowing that, we can journey on from here. Be a blessing to the women and children around you—and other guys, while you're at it. Add value to their lives. Give them a glimpse of a man who knows who he is and whose he is.

A guy like that isn't afraid. He laughs a lot.

He knows how it all ends, and—just like in the beginning—it will be very, very good.

DISCUSSION QUESTIONS

The Keeper of the Garden

1. When you first hear the phrase "a real man," what images come to mind? What does this man look like? What does he do for a living? What kind of vehicle does he drive? What does he wear and eat? What does he value the most in life?

2. Brant points back to Adam and says that the purpose of man is to be the "keeper of the garden." Describe in your own words what this title implies.

3. If you were forced to play one video game eight hours a day for thirty days, what would it be and why? (Brant's answer is *EA Sports FC*.) Does your game choice reveal anything about who you are and what you value?

4. Brant gave "Jake" as an example of a typical twenty-year-old. Jake thought he could do whatever he wanted if he didn't hurt anyone. Brant challenged that way of thinking: "He's harming himself and others by not being who he was created to be." Describe what you think is meant by this statement.

5. Discuss the meaning of the following statements and share your response to each one:

   A. Masculinity is about taking responsibility.

   B. Women see rescuing as attractive.

   C. Nobody admires a passive man or a blaming man.

   D. We need men who commit. Commitment means closing certain doors in favor of opening a better one.

Decision One: Forsake the Fake and Relish the Real

1. Brant calls sin a swindle. Describe when you bought a product because of some "cool" advertising and then it disappointed you. How did that make you feel? What did you do about it?

2. Give some examples of exaggerated fakes in our culture today. Which of them is the number one stimulus or temptation for your friends? Which is the number one stimulus or temptation for you?

3. Discuss your response to this statement: "Please don't waste your God-given desire for adventure and accomplishment by being a fake hero fighting fake injustices in fake worlds." Is Brant right that this can be a problem? If so, how?

4. From what you have learned in this section, list and discuss potential pitfalls of pornography and how it distorts what God has created you to be. How has pornography affected you?

5. Brant writes that to give up our addictions, we must have a bigger life vision. If you were to write a short statement summing up the man you want to be, what would it say? (Do you want to embrace the real over the fake? Do you want God's wisdom or the foolishness of the world?)

Decision Two: Protect the Vulnerable

1. The word "vulnerable" is used often in this book, and for good reason. What does it mean, and who are the vulnerable people in your school? At your work? On social media?

2. How do you think older generations view young men today? Are their assessments fair? Why or why not?

3. Have you ever taken any action to protect, help, or save someone? What happened?

4. In what ways do your friends or your generation in general seek to influence you to betray your role as a protector and keeper of the garden?

5. Brant writes, "You and I don't have to fit the stereotypes of what manly men look or sound like. What we do need to do is use whatever we have as great keepers of the garden to defend the defenseless." What can you do right now to defend the defenseless? Make a plan of action.

6. What qualities or attitudes of your parents, grandparents, or guardians do you want to hold on to as a man? What qualities or attitudes do you want to avoid?

Decision Three: Be Ambitious about the Right Things

1. Read Jesus' teaching of the wise and foolish builders in Matthew 7:24–27. What does Brant mean by "My sincerity does not change reality"? How does this statement relate to the Matthew parable?

2. Brant says that even terrible jobs make us serve people. What meaning does your work have to you, whether at school or on the job? How does it make you serve people? What occupation do you want to pursue someday? Talk about how you could help others in that occupation.

3. What are some things you think a husband might do to help his wife feel secure in life?

4. Psalm 23:1 says, "The LORD is my shepherd, I lack nothing." Is that believable to you—that you lack nothing? How might really believing that make life as a man better?

5. How do you want to leave your mark on this planet? How would you like to be known?

Decision Four: Make Women and Children Feel Safe, Not Threatened

1. Describe how most guys your age treat girls. Have you ever thought through how you should treat them? What do you do well? What do you need to work on?

2. How does what Jesus did for the woman caught in adultery (John 8) stand in stark contrast to how Adam protected—or didn't protect—Eve?

3. Read James 3:5–12. Write or discuss some encouraging things you need to say to the ones closest to you. Maybe they're things you have never said or you don't say enough. Then go say them to those people as soon as possible.

4. What about yourself do you need to protect your future wife from? What negative behaviors that scare you about yourself are you going to work on (e.g., anger or selfishness)?

5. What do you think about couples living together before marriage? Why is commitment so vital for a real man?

Decision Five: Choose Today Who You Will Become Tomorrow

1. Who you become is a direct result of what you pay attention to. Standing guard over your mind is vital. Read 2 Corinthians 10:5 and Colossians 3:12–17. What does it

mean to take every thought captive to make it obedient to Christ? What practical advice would you give someone struggling with their thought life?

2. Describe the challenge social media brings to your thought life. Take some time to think this through and consider how you can approach social media differently.

3. Which of the proverbs in the "Remember, Foolishness = Pain" chapter sticks out to you the most and why?

4. What do you want your life to be like in ten years? Thirty years? What do you think you will be like as an old man?

5. Brant writes, "Contentment brings freedom. Discontentment makes you dependent." What is he referring to?

6. We truly have nothing to fear. If God is for us, who can be against us? Read Romans 8:35–39. What words stick out the most and why? How do you feel after reading this passage?

Decision Six: Take Responsibility for Your Own Spiritual Life

1. What do you think about Brant's statement that what God is looking for from us is a believing, trusting loyalty? Does that ring true to you?

2. What might daily loyalty to God look like?

3. What role do feelings have in your spiritual life? Do you need to feel God's presence or experience "religious emotions" in order to be loyal to him? Why or why not?

4. "Whatever I do is fine as long as I'm not hurting someone else" is a common, modern idea. Why is it a mistaken one?

5. What did you think of Brant's car-prayer story? Can you give an example of a brutally honest prayer that you have prayed? Spend some time right now in brutally honest prayer. Ask God to help you be one of the young men we need.

Conclusion: A Final Word about Adam . . . and Us

1. What does the inclusion and description of Adam in Jesus' genealogy tell us about how God views us even when we fail?

2. Spend a few minutes (or more) discussing what you have learned in this study. What sticks out the most to you? Where do you need to make changes in your life? Describe the man you want to become.

ACKNOWLEDGMENTS

So thankful for my wife, Carolyn, and her encouragement as I struggle to write. I'm also thankful for our insightful and inspiring adult kids, Justice and Julia. And Zack, too, and now baby Scout, who at this writing is just a year old but has contributed to this book by being a most welcome and charming distraction.

Thank you to my brother, Darin Hansen, one of the kindest and most supportive people I've ever known.

And thank you, Patnacia Goodman at Baker, for seeing the need for such a book as this. Thank you, Jessica English, for making this book better with your incisive editing.

And thank you to the worldwide staff and supporters of CURE International Children's Hospitals: housekeepers, cooks, doctors, nurses, pastoral staff—everybody! So honored I get to be part of what God is doing through you. It's a beautiful thing.

NOTES

Masculinity Is about Taking Responsibility

1. Megan McCluskey, "Gillette Makes Waves with Controversial New Ad Highlighting 'Toxic Masculinity,'" *Time*, January 16, 2019, https://time.com/5503156/gillette-razors-toxic-masculinity.

2. Bible Study Tools, "Shamar," accessed October 5, 2021, https://www.biblestudytools.com/lexicons/hebrew/nas/shamar.html.

The Ancient Art of Blaming Other People

1. James Clear, "3 Ideas, 2 Quotes, 1 Question," November 5, 2020, email newsletter.

A Tale of Two Men . . . and Every Woman

1. The Star, "Malian Hero Scales Paris Building to Save Child," YouTube video, May 28, 2018, https://youtu.be/WISmbOw_bMk.

The Big Swindle

1. "She Is Broken & Being Repaired, Says Kazakh Bodybuilder Who Married His Sex Doll," DNA, December 26, 2020, https://www.dnaindia.com/world/report-she-is-broken-being-repaired-says-kazakh-bodybuilder-who-married-his-sex-doll-2864146.

2. Franki Cookney, "Sex Doll Sales Surge in Quarantine, but It's Not Just about Loneliness," *Forbes*, May 21, 2020, https://www.forbes.com/sites/frankicookney/2020/05/21/sex-doll-sales-surge-in-quarantine-but-its-not-just-about-loneliness.

3. "Our Technology," Robot Companion, accessed August 19, 2021, https://www.robotcompanion.ai/our-technology.

Let's Talk about "Supernormal" Traps

1. Deirdre Barrett, "Your Mind Is a Victim of Stone Age Instincts," *Wired*, July 5, 2015, https://www.wired.co.uk/article/stone-age-mind.
2. Barrett, "Your Mind Is a Victim."
3. Kurt Vonnegut, *God Bless You, Mr. Rosewater: A Novel* (New York: Dell, 1965), 109.

Video Games

1. Ishikawa Kiyoshi, "'Hikikomori': Social Recluses in the Shadows of an Aging Japan," Nippon.com, July 19, 2017, https://www.nippon.com/en/currents/d00332.
2. Laurence Butet-Roch, "Pictures Reveal the Isolated Lives of Japan's Recluses," *National Geographic*, February 14, 2018, https://www.nationalgeographic.com/photography/proof/2018/february/japan-hikikomori-isolation-society/#close.

Here's Some Good News about Pornography. No, Really.

1. Dr. Carlo Floresta, "Project AndroLIFE, Health and Sex" (lecture), 2014, https://www.yourbrainonporn.com/porn-induced-sexual-dysfunctions/experts-who-recognize-porn-induced-sexual-dysfunctions-along-with-relevant-studies/pdf-of-a-lecture-by-carlo-foresta-urology-professor-2014.
2. Dr. Philip Zimbardo and Nikita Duncan, "The Demise of Guys: How Video Games and Porn Are Ruining a Generation," CNN, May 24, 2012, https://www.cnn.com/2012/05/23/health/living-well/demise-of-guys/index.html.
3. Gary Wilson, "The Great Porn Experiment," TEDx Talks, May 16, 2012, YouTube video, 4:45, https://www.youtube.com/watch?v=wSF82AwSDiU.
4. Wilson, "The Great Porn Experiment," 16:21.
5. K_B, "Day 319, the biggest changes I've experienced so far in my life . . . ," Reddit, February 1, 2021, https://www.reddit.com/r/NoFap/comments/kkk1ub/day_319_the_biggest_changes_ive_experienced_so.
6. NinjaRabbIT09, "Feeling so much better," Reddit, July 1, 2019, https://www.reddit.com/r/NoFap/comments/9pobve/feeling_so_much_better.
7. MiddlewaysOfTruth-2, comment on Startagain2020, "I guess watching porn fills us with hatred," Reddit, February 1, 2021, https://www.reddit.com/r/NoFap/comments/kkgifs/i_guess_watching_porn_fills_us_with_hatred.
8. GiraffePuncher69, "90 days—I did it," Reddit, February 1, 2021, https://www.reddit.com/r/NoFap/comments/kk8w8q/90_days_i_did_it.

One More Short Chapter about Sex

1. "The State of STDs—Infographic," CDC, April 11, 2023, https://www.cdc.gov/std/statistics/infographic.htm.
2. "U.S. Statistics," HIV.gov, October 27, 2022, https://www.hiv.gov/hiv-basics/overview/data-and-trends/statistics/.
3. John Elflein, "Number of Legal Abortions Reported in the U.S. from 1973 to 2020," Statista, December 15, 2022, https://www.statista.com/statistics/185274/number-of-legal-abortions-in-the-us-since-2000/.

4. Eric Barker, "What Makes More Money: Sports or Porn?," Business Insider, May 4, 2012, https://www.businessinsider.com/what-makes-more-money-sports-or-porn-2012-5#:~:text=Worldwide%2C%20pornography%20is%20reported%20to.

5. Alexis Kleinman, "Porn Sites Get More Visitors Each Month Than Netflix, Amazon and Twitter Combined," HuffPost, December 6, 2017, https://www.huff post.com/entry/internet-porn-stats_n_3187682#:~:text=Porn%20Sites%20Get%20More%20Visitors.

6. Vicki Larson, "Does Porn Watching Lead to Divorce?," HuffPost, May 29, 2011, https://www.huffpost.com/entry/porn-and-divorce_b_861987.

Your Neighborhood Should Be Safer Simply Because You're There

1. Riaan Grobler, "'I Couldn't Imagine Ever Doing Anything Like That'—Man Who Tackled Alleged Restaurant Child Snatcher," News24, September 14, 2020, https://www.news24.com/news24/southafrica/news/i-never-imagined-doing-some thing-like-this-man-who-tackled-alleged-restaurant-child-snatcher-20200914.

2. Grobler, "'I Couldn't Imagine.'"

3. "Statistical Briefing Book," Office of Juvenile Justice and Delinquency Prevention, accessed July 27, 2023, https://www.ojjdp.gov/ojstatbb/crime/ucr.asp?table_in=1.

4. Health Encyclopedia, "Understanding the Teen Brain," University of Rochester Medical Center, accessed July 27, 2023, https://www.urmc.rochester.edu /encyclopedia/content.aspx?ContentTypeID=1&ContentID=3051#:~:text=The %20rational%20part%20of%20a.

The Ultimate Betrayal

1. "5 Teenagers Save 2 Small Children after Sled Somehow Ends Up in Frigid New Jersey Pond," CBS New York, December 20, 2020, https://newyork.cbslocal .com/2020/12/20/teenagers-save-children-after-sled-goes-into-pond-atlantic-high lands-new-jersey.

A Quick Word

1. Rachel Bowman, "Viral Video Shows Man Jump from Top of Pennybacker Bridge," CBS Austin, November 28, 2020, https://cbsaustin.com/news/local/viral -video-shows-man-jump-from-top-of-pennybacker-bridge.

How to Treat Women: The Bridger Master Class

1. Bri Lamm, "'If Someone Had to Die, I Thought It Should Be Me'—Chris Hemsworth, Hugh Jackman & Chris Evans Praise 6-Year-Old Hero Who Saved Sister from Dog Attack," Faithit, July 16, 2020, https://faithit.com/if-someone-had -to-die-i-thought-it-should-be-me-chris-hemsworth-chris-evans-praise-bridger -save-sister-dog-attack.

Protect Them . . . from You

1. Richard D. Phillips, *The Masculine Mandate* (Sanford, FL: Reformation Trust Publishing, 2010), 118–19.

Attention Is Everything

1. Dallas Willard, *Renovation of the Heart: Putting On the Character of Christ* (Colorado Springs: The Navigators, 2014), 16.

2. Lisa Magloff, "Repetition as an Advertisement Technique," CHRON, February 1, 2019, https://smallbusiness.chron.com/repetition-advertisement-technique -24437.html.

Remember, Foolishness = Pain

1. If I could edit the Bible, I'd include more bears. But you're not supposed to edit the Bible, so never mind. But still.

2. Eva Krockow, "How Many Decisions Do We Make Each Day?," *Psychology Today*, September 27, 2018, https://www.psychologytoday.com/us/blog/stretching -theory/201809/how-many-decisions-do-we-make-each-day.

Walmart Shopping Cart Attack Guy Never Set Out to Be Walmart Shopping Cart Attack Guy

1. Frances Parkinson Keyes, "A Story of Friendly Flags," *Good Housekeeping*, May 1925, 164.

What God Is Looking For

1. J. R. R. Tolkien, *The Fellowship of the Ring* (Boston: Houghton Mifflin, 1988), 150.

BRANT HANSEN is a bestselling author, radio host, and advocate for healing children with correctible disabilities through CURE International Children's Hospitals. His award-winning radio show, *The Brant Hansen Show*, is syndicated on top stations nationwide. His podcast with his producer, *The Brant and Sherri Oddcast*, has been downloaded more than fifteen million times. The author of *Unoffendable*, *The Truth about Us*, and *The Men We Need*, Hansen lives in South Florida with his wife, Carolyn. Learn more at www.BrantHansen.com and find out about CURE at www.Cure.org.

Connect with Brant
www.BrantHansen.com

f @BrantHansenPage   **X** @BrantHansen

Thank you for reading this book.

I want to leave you with a challenge (and if you can't do it or don't want to do it, that's okay).

Here it is: *Help us heal kids and tell them and their families how much they are loved by God.*

There are millions of kids with disabilities that are correctable. They're subject to abuse and intense rejection. They're often considered cursed. But getting access to surgery changes everything for them.

That's what CURE does! This has been my passion for years. I've visited these hospitals and met these kids, these families, these doctors . . . and this looks like Jesus to me.

Kids can walk and skip and dance and run for the first time in their lives! Moms and dads are crying with joy!

This is what I wish we followers of Jesus were known for: healing. **Please consider jumping online right now (cure.org) and becoming a CURE Hero.**

And if you want some amazing inspiration (and to see where your money is going!), check out this documentary on Amazon Prime or YouTube.

WINNER
BEST INTERNATIONAL DOCUMENTARY
GREAT LAKES CHRISTIAN
FILM FESTIVAL
2018

NOMINEE
BEST INSPIRATIONAL DOCUMENTARY
INTERNATIONAL CHRISTIAN
FILM FESTIVAL
2018

WINNER
BEST DOCUMENTARY SUPPORTING A
CHRISTIAN WORLDVIEW
FILM FESTIVAL
2018

CURE INTERNATIONAL PRESENTS

MODERN DAY
MIRACLES